Optimizing the Role of Military Behavioral Health Technicians

A Survey of Behavioral Health Technicians and
Mental Health Providers

KIMBERLY A. HEPNER, STEPHANIE BROOKS HOLLIDAY,
ALLYSON D. GITTENS, IRINEO C. CABREROS,
CHERYL K. MONTEMAYOR, HAROLD ALAN PINCUS

Prepared for the Psychological Health Center of Excellence
Approved for public release; distribution unlimited

RAND NATIONAL DEFENSE RESEARCH INSTITUTE

For more information on this publication, visit **www.rand.org/t/RRA1191-1**.

About RAND

The RAND Corporation is a research organization that develops solutions to public policy challenges to help make communities throughout the world safer and more secure, healthier and more prosperous. RAND is nonprofit, nonpartisan, and committed to the public interest. To learn more about RAND, visit www.rand.org.

Research Integrity

Our mission to help improve policy and decisionmaking through research and analysis is enabled through our core values of quality and objectivity and our unwavering commitment to the highest level of integrity and ethical behavior. To help ensure our research and analysis are rigorous, objective, and nonpartisan, we subject our research publications to a robust and exacting quality-assurance process; avoid both the appearance and reality of financial and other conflicts of interest through staff training, project screening, and a policy of mandatory disclosure; and pursue transparency in our research engagements through our commitment to the open publication of our research findings and recommendations, disclosure of the source of funding of published research, and policies to ensure intellectual independence. For more information, visit www.rand.org/about/principles.

RAND's publications do not necessarily reflect the opinions of its research clients and sponsors.

Published by the RAND Corporation, Santa Monica, Calif.
© 2022 RAND Corporation
RAND® is a registered trademark.

Library of Congress Cataloging-in-Publication Data is available for this publication.
ISBN: 978-1-9774-0706-1

About This Report

Behavioral health technicians (BHTs) are an important part of the Military Health System's (MHS's) mental health care workforce. These enlisted service members who work alongside licensed mental health providers (MHPs) serve as care extenders, helping the MHS improve the efficiency and effectiveness of the behavioral health care that it provides. The U.S. Department of Defense's Psychological Health Center of Excellence (PHCoE) asked the RAND Corporation to assess the current functional operation and utilization of BHTs across the MHS and to develop actionable recommendations for optimizing their engagement. Previous RAND research examined the selection criteria for the BHT career field and training available to BHTs. It found inconsistencies in how BHTs were integrated across the force, recommending greater standardization in selection criteria, curriculum, on-the-job training, and professional development opportunities for BHTs. This follow-on report presents the results of a survey of a representative sample of BHTs and MHPs, who provided additional insights on how BHTs function in practice, how prepared they were to fulfill these roles, and what barriers they encountered.

The research reported here was completed in March 2021 and underwent security review with the sponsor and the Defense Office of Prepublication and Security Review before public release.

RAND National Security Research Division

This research was sponsored by PHCoE and conducted within the Forces and Resources Policy Center of the RAND National Security Research Division (NSRD), which operates the National Defense Research Institute (NDRI), a federally funded research and development center sponsored by the Office of the Secretary of Defense, the Joint Staff, the Unified Combatant Commands, the Navy, the Marine Corps, the defense agencies, and the defense intelligence enterprise.

For more information on the RAND Forces and Resources Policy Center, see www.rand.org/nsrd/frp.html or contact the director (contact information is provided on the webpage).

Acknowledgments

We gratefully acknowledge the support of our project sponsor, the U.S. Department of Defense Psychological Health Center of Excellence, including TSgt Krista Rehmert, Timothy Hoyt, Sgt Bradley Blair, MAJ Mary Markivich, and MAJ Aimee Ruscio. In addition, we acknowledge the ongoing support and valuable input we received from the Defense Health Agency's Behavioral Health Technician Work Group. The surveys benefited from reviews by several experts, including Carrie Farmer, Chaitra Hardison, COL Chris Ivany, Tracy Krueger, and Lisa Meredith. We also thank the staff at Davis Research for their assistance in fielding the provider survey, particularly Jason Kerns, who oversaw that effort. We appreciate the valuable insights we received from our reviewers, Carrie Farmer and Stacey Young-McCaughan. We addressed their constructive critiques as part of RAND's rigorous quality assurance process to improve the quality of this report. We also thank Lauren Skrabala and Rosa Maria Torres for their assistance in preparing this report and Terry Marsh for overseeing human subjects and regulatory approvals for the project. Finally, we extend our gratitude to the more than 500 BHTs and 600 licensed MHPs who participated in our survey.

Summary

Behavioral health technicians (BHTs), enlisted service members with the technical training to work alongside licensed mental health providers (MHPs), are an important part of the Military Health System (MHS) mental health care workforce. They serve as care extenders, helping the MHS improve the efficiency and effectiveness of the behavioral health care that it provides. However, each service branch has different training requirements for BHTs, making it difficult to identify common qualifications across the BHT workforce and ensure that the MHS is making the best use of their skills. The U.S. Department of Defense's (DoD's) Psychological Health Center of Excellence asked the RAND Corporation to assess the current functional operation and utilization of BHTs and to develop actionable recommendations for optimizing their engagement across the MHS.

Previous RAND research examined the selection criteria for the BHT career field and the training available to these personnel. It found inconsistencies in how BHTs were integrated across the force, recommending greater standardization in selection criteria, curriculum, on-the-job training (OJT), and professional development opportunities (Holliday et al., 2019). This follow-on report presents the results of what might be the largest survey of BHTs and MHPs in the MHS ever conducted.

The goal of this project was to assess current practice patterns, BHTs' training needs, barriers and facilitators to better integrating BHTs into clinical practice, and potential steps that the MHS can take to optimize BHTs' contributions to the health and readiness of the force. We developed separate but largely parallel surveys for BHTs and MHPs on BHT roles, responsibilities, and training. The parallel sets of questions we posed to these groups provided useful insights and allowed us to compare perspectives on BHTs' roles and responsibilities, the frequency with which BHTs performed clinical tasks, the training and supervision they received, barriers to their effective integration into clinical settings, BHTs' satisfaction with their work and fit with the career field, and MHPs' satisfaction with BHTs' work. The survey also elicited perceptions on a series of potential changes to BHT practice that could improve how BHTs are integrated into clinical settings.

We drew eligible survey participants from the Health Manpower Personnel Data System and sent our survey to active-duty BHTs in the Army, Navy, and Air Force, as well as to active-duty and DoD government civilian MHPs who had worked with a BHT in the previous 12 months, including licensed psychiatrists, mental health nurse practitioners, doctoral-level psychologists, and master's-level providers (i.e., social workers and master's-level psychologists). In total, we surveyed 538 BHTs and 685 MHPs (adjusted response rate: 42 percent for BHTs; 37 percent for MHPs).

Nearly 70 percent of BHTs were assigned to in-garrison military treatment facilities, with about 16 percent assigned to in-garrison operational units. Few BHTs were deployed at the time of the survey, and relatively few BHTs or MHPs reported having deployed in the previous 12 months. It was most common for BHTs and MHPs to be working in outpatient mental health and substance use treatment settings. Relatively fewer BHTs and MHPs were serving in other clinical settings or specialty programs. About half of BHTs and MHPs reported interacting with patients across multiple settings. BHTs tended to work with multiple MHPs, and it was common for them to support psychiatrists, psychiatric nurse practitioners, doctoral-level psychologists, and social workers. However, slightly fewer than half of the MHPs surveyed indicated that they were supervising a BHT at the time of the survey, with doctoral-level psychologists and prescribing providers being more likely to indicate that they did so.

Across the MHS, BHTs Varied in Their Responsibilities and How They Applied Their Skills

BHTs engage in a wide variety of tasks, including screening and assessment, psychosocial interventions, treatment planning and monitoring, and outreach and resilience activities. Both BHTs and MHPs reported that BHTs perform screening and assessment activities most often, but there was variation in the amount of time they spent on other clinical tasks, depending on their branch of service and current assignment. About half of BHTs who had deployed in the previous 12 months indicated that they performed more screening and assessment tasks, psychosocial interventions, and outreach and resilience tasks and fewer treatment planning/monitoring activities while serving in a deployed setting. Furthermore, about 90 percent of BHTs and MHPs reported substantial variability in BHT skills, even within the same rank. This finding aligns with our previous research finding that BHTs have a broad range of skills, but not all of these personnel have the same opportunity for ongoing training to maintain and develop their skills.

BHTs reported spending about one-third of their time on patient care activities in a typical week—but also an equivalent amount of time on administrative clinic responsibilities and nearly one-quarter of their time on nonclinical responsibilities. Previous research has suggested that BHTs might not spend a substantial portion of their duty hours on clinical tasks, given other competing demands (Nielson, 2016), and our results support that conclusion. Findings also suggest that BHTs across the force are not getting consistent opportunities to practice some clinical skills and may find themselves unprepared to perform certain patient care tasks when they change settings or assignments. BHTs who spent more time on patient care reported greater satisfaction, so more time spent on administrative tasks could affect their engagement with their work or longevity in the career field.

BHTs and MHPs Differed in Their Perceptions of BHT Proficiency and the Frequency with Which BHTs Performed Various Tasks

Although BHTs and MHPs generally agreed that BHTs were most proficient at screening and assessment-related tasks, they differed in their perceptions of BHTs' level of proficiency. Specifically, 97 percent of BHTs indicated that they could conduct risk assessments with no assistance or conduct them with no assistance and train someone else on the task. However, only 43 percent of MHPs agreed. There were similar significant discrepancies in reported proficiency across all the clinical tasks in our survey. A reason for this variation could be unrealistic expectations on the part of MHPs, or BHTs might be unaware of their weaknesses on certain tasks or the expected skill level for these tasks. The survey results also indicated that MHPs might lack familiarity with the range of tasks BHTs can perform. Indeed, BHTs and MHPs varied in their reports of the frequency with which BHTs performed certain tasks, and more than three-quarters of MHPs indicated that further education on how best to utilize BHTs' skills could improve the effectiveness of BHTs in the MHS. Efforts to address this mismatch in perceptions will be important. MHPs who perceived BHTs as more proficient were more satisfied with BHTs' performance, and MHPs who have had a positive experience with BHTs might be likelier to integrate them more meaningfully into clinical tasks.

BHTs' Satisfaction with Their Work Was Associated with Increased Time on Patient Care and Receiving Adequate Supervision

About two-thirds of BHTs reported satisfaction with their military job and the quality of their supervisor. Our findings suggest that the nature of BHT responsibilities contributes to their satisfaction. BHTs who reported spending more time on clinical tasks—rather than administrative or unit responsibilities—were more satisfied with their work. Relatedly, BHTs who felt more proficient completing clinical tasks were also more satisfied. We also found that BHTs who reported that they were a good fit for their job were more satisfied.

BHTs and MHPs reported that classroom instruction for BHTs was generally adequate, but many suggested that time spent on continuing education and supervision was inadequate. In turn, we found that BHTs who reported receiving adequate supervision had higher levels of satisfaction, and MHPs who perceived supervision to be adequate were more satisfied with BHTs' performance.

BHTs Encountered Barriers to Developing and Using Their Skills

To gain a better understanding of the factors that could affect the types of roles that BHTs fulfill, including the extent to which they are integrated into clinical responsibilities, we asked BHTs and MHPs about barriers to effective BHT practice. Among both BHTs and MHPs, the most commonly endorsed barrier was variability in BHT skills, even among those with the same rank. Other frequently cited barriers related to MHP expectations and familiarity with BHT skills, as well as how BHTs' responsibilities were allocated and the level of supervision they received. The majority of BHTs and MHPs agreed that providers would be more comfortable sharing clinical tasks with BHTs if BHTs had a credential.

Nearly 80 percent of MHPs saw a need for more-systematic supervision for BHTs to effectively provide clinical care. In comparison, only 45 percent of BHTs saw a need for more-systematic supervision. However, many BHTs indicated that MHPs do not have enough time to invest in ongoing supervision and training. This suggests that while MHPs see supervision as key to BHT skill development, finding time to provide this supervision may still be an issue.

Some barriers were endorsed less frequently. Only a modest proportion of BHTs and MHPs indicated that BHTs might feel more comfortable receiving OJT from a senior enlisted BHT than from an MHP. This suggests that it is not *who* provides the supervision that matters but, rather, that intentional time is set aside to provide supervision. In addition, relatively fewer BHTs and MHPs indicated that MHPs were concerned that they would not receive credit for care provided alongside a BHT.

There Are Opportunities to Improve BHT Training, Including Through Continuing Education and Supervision

Our survey asked about potential changes to BHT practice and how MHPs integrate these personnel into clinical settings. Our goal was to identify how BHTs could contribute more effectively to providing high-quality behavioral health care to service members across the MHS. The vast majority of BHTs (90 percent) agreed that they should be provided with ongoing professional development opportunities. Such a change could address the perceived variability in BHT skills that our survey highlighted. BHTs also indicated that they could be more effective if they received training to implement approaches that are effective across multiple psychiatric diagnoses and to provide evidence-based psychotherapies (EBPs) to lower-risk patients.

MHPs similarly saw a need for more professional development opportunities for BHTs, more education for MHPs on how to integrate BHTs into clinical practice, and improved policies defining BHTs' responsibilities.

There were several differences between BHTs and MHPs in their perceptions of which changes could be most beneficial, however. The largest difference pertained to the possibility of training BHTs to implement EBPs with clinically complex patients; BHTs overall found this option to be more promising than MHPs. This difference and others echoed differences in perceptions of BHTs' training and skills. For example, both BHTs and MHPs reported that BHTs do not currently administer EBPs very often, so this could help explain why fewer MHPs found this change in BHT practice less essential than BHTs, who might want further training in this area.

These perspectives on potential changes to BHT practice point to several solutions that could improve opportunities for BHTs to apply their skills. For example, a structured approach to supervising BHTs could have benefits in addressing MHPs' reservations about sharing clinical tasks with uncredentialed BHTs. One such approach is a tiered supervision model, in which newer MHPs supervise BHTs. In turn, a more-established MHP provides supervision to the newer MHP, including guidance on how to effectively supervise a BHT, resulting in skill development for both the new MHP and the BHT.

Recommendations

Building on these findings and the data we collected on BHT selection, curriculum, and training in the first phase of this study, we identified four primary opportunities to improve how BHTs are integrated into clinical settings and how the MHS can help them maintain and make the best use of their skills.

Recommendation 1. Standardize Expectations for BHTs' Scope of Practice and Educate Providers on BHT Roles

Our findings make it clear that BHTs can play a wide variety of roles. In many ways, this is by design: BHT technical training covers a broad range of clinical topics and skills, and service branch policy documents outline a similarly broad range of BHT responsibilities. However, this also means that BHTs' skills may be applied in various ways across settings and supervisors, potentially leading to uneven skill development.

One way to reverse this trend would be to standardize expectations for BHTs' scope of practice, including issuing specific guidelines regarding the skills that BHTs are expected to maintain regardless of setting, with a focus on high-frequency tasks, such as risk assessments, intake interviews, and administering and scoring behavioral health symptom measures. This could be articulated in formal policy or guidance documents, but it should nonetheless also address low-frequency or out-of-scope BHT tasks, such as those related to the provision of psychotherapy or working with high-acuity patients. Ongoing education for MHPs in supervisory roles would promote greater consistency in how BHTs' skills are applied across the MHS. Finally, there is a need to examine how BHT time is allocated between administrative and clinical tasks, with the goal of providing adequate opportunities to exercise clinical skills. Our survey results suggest that providing adequate time for clinical activities could enhance BHTs' job satisfaction.

Recommendation 2. Provide Clinical Support Tools to Structure BHT Tasks

BHTs and MHPs had vastly different perspectives on BHT proficiency in performing certain clinical tasks. This highlights a potential need for more clinical support tools, with our survey respondents recommending the use of templates, checklists, or forms to structure clinical tasks. These tools could target, for example, the most frequently performed BHT tasks or support BHTs' training in treatment approaches that can be used across multiple psychiatric diagnoses. Standardized tools would have the added benefit of aligning expectations for BHT performance across settings and supervisors.

As suggested in our prior report, manualized or structured interventions that have been adapted for non-MHP mental health personnel could be adapted for use by BHTs, such as interventions that incorporate problem-solving therapy or motivational enhancement therapy (Holliday et al., 2019). Our findings suggest that MHPs would be receptive to training to support

BHTs in implementing transdiagnostic approaches or EBPs with low-risk patients.

Recommendation 3. Standardize and Communicate Expectations for Supervision Through Policy Guidance

Seventy-eight percent of MHPs indicated that there is a need for more-structured supervision of BHTs, while 66 percent of BHTs indicated that MHPs had limited time to invest in supervision and training. Inadequate supervision can deprive BHTs of opportunities to develop and practice their clinical skills. As part of efforts to promote standardized expectations for BHTs' skills and performance, it would be helpful to specify expectations or requirements for MHPs who supervise BHTs. Supervision can include a wide range of activities, from direct observation to cofacilitating sessions and staffing cases after BHTs provide one-on-one services. There has also been little specificity about the amount of time BHTs should spend in supervision with MHPs.

As health care services become integrated under the Defense Health Agency, there are opportunities to create policies related to supervision. Proposed standards address the amount of time that should be allocated to supervision each week and what modalities qualify as formal supervision (versus informal consultation). Such documents should also account for necessary adaptations for deployed environments, where BHTs may be expected to operate more autonomously and sometimes while geographically separated from their supervising provider.

Recommendation 4. Expand Continuing Education for BHTs, Such as Through the Development of a BHT-Specific Continuing Education Curriculum

The initial BHT technical training curriculum prioritizes breadth over depth. This makes continuing education and on-the-job skill development critical components of successful progression along the BHT career path. Indeed, the BHTs and MHPs we surveyed indicated that time spent on initial BHT training was adequate, but they also indicated that there was a need for more ongoing training opportunities. Notably, Air Force BHTs and

MHPs were less likely to indicate that too little time was allocated to BHT continuing education, likely reflecting the fact that the Air Force has the most standardized continuing education curriculum for BHTs. It is possible that the Air Force could serve as a model for the other services.

Conclusion

Our survey results indicated that, across the MHS, there was significant variation in BHTs' responsibilities and the tasks they performed, as well as how they were integrated into clinical settings. Importantly, BHTs reported greater job satisfaction when engaging in activities related to patient care, so more opportunities to perform these types of tasks—combined with adequate supervision and greater standardization in continuing education opportunities—could increase engagement and retention among BHTs. These personnel reported that only about a third of their time was spent on patient care responsibilities, indicating that BHTs might not be getting practice in these important skills and highlighting opportunities to better use their skills and training. Greater standardization of the BHT role and requirements related to supervision and continuing education might also increase MHPs' comfort integrating BHTs into clinical tasks. By addressing these factors, BHTs will be better prepared to support the mission of the MHS and to enhance behavioral health support for service members.

Contents

About This Report.. iii
Summary v
Figures and Tables... xix

CHAPTER ONE
Introduction 1
   Overview 1
   Behavioral Health Technicians in the Military Health System.............. 2
   Survey of Behavioral Health Technicians and Mental Health
       Providers... 11
   Organization of This Report 12

CHAPTER TWO
Methods... 13
   Identifying Eligible Survey Participants and Sampling Strategies 13
   Survey Development and Domains....................................... 15
   Survey Operations 17
   Data Analyses.. 19
   Summary... 24

CHAPTER THREE
Demographic, Service, and Practice Characteristics...................... 25
   Demographic and Service Characteristics................................ 25
   Practice Settings and Roles 30
   Summary... 34

CHAPTER FOUR
BHT Responsibilities and Clinical Tasks................................. 37
   Breakdown of BHT Responsibilities..................................... 37
   Frequency of BHT Clinical Tasks....................................... 39
   Summary... 50

CHAPTER FIVE

Perceptions of BHT Proficiency..53

BHT and MHP Perceptions of BHT Proficiency............................53

Relationship Between Frequency and Perceived Proficiency 63

Changes in Responsibilities During Deployment 65

Out-of-Scope Responsibilities..66

Summary..71

CHAPTER SIX

Training and Supervision 75

Perceived Adequacy of BHT Training..75

Perceived Adequacy of BHT Supervision...................................81

Summary..84

CHAPTER SEVEN

Barriers to Effective BHT Practice 87

BHT Perspectives on Barriers to BHT Practice.............................87

MHP Perspectives on Barriers to BHT Practice............................90

BHT and MHP Agreement on Barriers to Effective Practice..............92

Summary..96

CHAPTER EIGHT

Satisfaction..99

BHT Satisfaction 99

MHP Satisfaction 103

BHTs' Fit for the Job 106

Summary... 110

CHAPTER NINE

Perceptions of Changes to BHT Practice 113

BHT Perspectives of Changes to BHT Practice........................... 113

MHP Perspectives on Changes to BHT Practice.......................... 116

BHT and MHP Agreement on Potential Changes to BHT Practice...... 119

Summary... 122

CHAPTER TEN

Conclusions and Recommendations. 125

    Strengths and Limitations 125

    Key Findings. 126

    Recommendations 129

    Summary. 134

APPENDIXES

A. **Survey Sampling and Weighting**. 135

B. **Survey Development and Domains**. 145

C. **BHT Survey**. 157

D. **MHP Survey** 187

E. **Supplementary Analyses** 215

Abbreviations. 239

References 241

Figures and Tables

Figures

3.1. BHT and MHP Recent Deployments, Overall and by Service Branch 27
3.2. BHT and MHP Treatment Settings 31
3.3. MHP Practice Attributes, Overall and by Service Branch 34
3.4. MHP Practice Attributes, by Provider Type 35
4.1. Percentage of Time BHTs Spent on Activities in a Typical Week 38
4.2. Percentage of BHTs Who Reported Performing Tasks Often or Very Often 40
4.3. Percentage of MHPs Who Reported That BHTs Performed Tasks Often or Very Often 45
4.4. Top Five Discrepancies Between BHT-Reported and MHP-Reported Frequency with Which BHTs Performed Tasks 49
5.1. Percentage of BHTs Who Reported Ability to Perform a Task with No Assistance and to Train Someone Else on That Task 55
5.2. Percentage of MHPs Who Reported That BHTs Could Perform a Task with No Assistance and Could Train Someone Else on That Task 59
5.3. Top Five Discrepancies Between BHT and MHP Perceptions of BHT Proficiency 64
5.4. BHT-Reported Frequency of Tasks While Deployed 67
6.1. Percentage of BHTs Who Reported Insufficient BHT Time in Training, Overall and by Service Branch 76
6.2. Percentage of BHTs Who Reported Insufficient BHT Time in Training, by Time Spent on Patient Care Activities 79
6.3. Percentage of MHPs Who Reported Insufficient BHT Time in Training, Overall and by Service Branch 80
6.4. Percentage of BHTs and MHPs Who Indicated That BHTs Did Not Receive Adequate Supervision, Overall and by Service Branch 82

7.1. Percentage of BHTs Who Agreed or Strongly Agreed with Statements About Barriers to Effective BHT Practice............88

7.2. Percentage of MHPs Who Agreed or Strongly Agreed with Statements About Barriers to Effective BHT Practice............91

7.3. Barriers with Highest Agreement Between BHTs and MHPs...93

7.4. Barriers with Largest Discrepancies Between BHTs and MHPs..95

8.1. Percentage of BHTs Who Indicated That They Were Satisfied or Very Satisfied, Overall and by Service Branch.... 100

8.2. Percentage of BHTs Who Indicated That They Were Satisfied or Very Satisfied, by Perceived Adequacy of Supervision 101

8.3. Percentage of BHTs Satisfied or Very Satisfied with Their Work, by Time Spent on Patient Care 102

8.4. MHP Satisfaction, by Supervision-Related Factors 105

8.5. Mean Ratings of Person-Job Fit, Overall and by Service Branch.. 107

8.6. Mean Ratings of Person-Job Fit, by BHT Satisfaction with Military Job... 108

8.7. Ratings of Person-Job Fit, by BHT Satisfaction with Quality of Supervisor 109

9.1. Percentage of BHTs Who Agreed Very Much or Extremely with Potential Changes 114

9.2. Percentage of MHPs Who Agreed Very Much or Extremely with Potential Changes 117

9.3. Potential Changes to BHT Practice with Highest Agreement Between BHTs and MHPs............................ 120

9.4. Potential Changes to BHT Practice with Largest Discrepancies Between BHTs and MHPs 121

E.1. Frequency with Which BHTs Reported Performing Clinical Tasks 216

E.2. MHP-Reported Frequency with Which BHTs Performed Clinical Tasks 217

E.3. BHT Self-Reported Proficiency in Performing Clinical Tasks.. 218

E.4. MHP-Reported BHT Proficiency in Performing Clinical Tasks.. 219

E.5. BHT and MHP Perceptions of Supervision Adequacy, Overall and by Service Branch.................................... 220

E.6.   BHT Perceptions of Barriers to Effective BHT Practice........ 221
E.7.   MHP Perceptions of Barriers to Effective BHT Practice....... 224
E.8.   BHT Satisfaction, Overall and by Service Branch.............. 229
E.9.   BHT Satisfaction with Their Work, by Time Spent on
        Patient Care... 229
E.10.   MHP Satisfaction with BHTs' Performance, Overall and by
        Service Branch 230
E.11.   BHT Perceptions of Potential Changes to BHT Practice....... 232
E.12.   MHP Perceptions of Potential Changes to BHT Practice...... 234

Tables

1.1.   Summary of Key Challenges to the Effective Training and
        Use of BHTs 9
2.1.   Survey Domains and Number of Items........................... 16
2.2.   Final BHT Analytic Sample Compared with the BHT
        Population 21
2.3.   Final MHP Analytic Sample Compared with the MHP
        Population 21
3.1.   Characteristics of BHTs and MHPs Included in the Analytic
        Sample... 26
3.2.   BHT Time in Practice, Overall and by Service Branch.......... 28
3.3.   MHP Time in Practice in the MHS, Overall and by Service
        Branch... 29
3.4.   MHP Time in Practice in the MHS, by Provider Type 29
3.5.   BHT Current Assignment, Overall and by Service Branch...... 32
3.6.   Providers Supported by BHTs, Overall and by Service
        Branch... 33
4.1.   BHT-Reported Frequency of Tasks, Overall and by Service
        Branch... 42
4.2.   Association Between BHT-Reported Frequency of Tasks
        and Practice Attributes 43
4.3.   MHP-Reported Frequency of Tasks, Overall and by Service
        Branch... 46
5.1.   BHT-Reported Proficiency in Performing Tasks, Overall
        and by Service Branch 56
5.2.   Association Between BHT-Reported Proficiency in
        Performing Tasks and Practice Attributes 57

5.3.   MHP-Reported BHT Proficiency in Performing Tasks,
        Overall and by Service Branch.......................................60
5.4.   Association Between MHP-Reported BHT Proficiency in
        Performing Tasks and Practice Attributes 62
5.5.   Association Between Frequency of Tasks and Proficiency.......65
5.6.   Type of Deployment, Overall and by Service Branch............66
5.7.   Settings in Which BHTs Practiced Outside of Scope.............68
5.8.   Qualitative Coding of Out-of-Scope Activities....................69
6.1.   Percentage of BHTs Reporting Insufficient BHT Time in
        Training, by Years in Practice.....................................78
8.1.   Percentage of MHPs Satisfied or Very Satisfied with BHTs,
        Overall and by Service Branch................................... 103
A.1.   Number of BHTs, by Service Branch............................. 135
A.2.   Number of MHPs in the Provider Population, by Stratum 136
A.3.   Proportion of BHTs Sampled from Each Service Branch 137
A.4.   Proportion of MHPs Sampled from Each Stratum............. 137
A.5.   BHT Raw Response Rates, by Service Branch 138
A.6.   MHP Raw Response Rates, by Stratum.......................... 139
A.7.   BHT Analytic Cohort, by Service Branch....................... 141
A.8.   MHP Analytic Cohort, by Stratum 141
B.1.   BHT and MHP Survey Content and Sources 152
B.2.   BHT Task Subscores and Specific Tasks Within Each
        Subscore... 155
E.1.   BHT Perceptions of Barriers to Effective BHT Practice,
        by Service Branch.. 222
E.2.   BHT Perceptions of Barriers to Effective BHT Practice,
        by Time in Practice.. 223
E.3.   MHP Perceptions of Barriers to Effective BHT Practice,
        by Service Branch.. 225
E.4.   MHP Perceptions of Barriers to Effective BHT Practice,
        by Provider Type... 226
E.5.   MHP Perceptions of Barriers to Effective BHT Practice,
        by Time in Practice in the MHS 227
E.6.   MHP Perceptions of Barriers to Effective BHT Practice,
        by Military Status.. 228
E.7.   BHT Perceptions of Potential Changes to BHT Practice,
        by Service Branch.. 231
E.8.   BHT Perceptions of Potential Changes to BHT Practice,
        by Time in Practice.. 233

E.9. MHP Perceptions of Potential Changes to BHT Practice, by Service Branch... 235

E.10. MHP Perceptions of Potential Changes to BHT Practice, by Time in Practice in the MHS.................................... 236

E.11. MHP Perceptions of Potential Changes to BHT Practice, by Military Status... 237

E.12. MHP Perceptions of Potential Changes to BHT Practice, by Provider Type... 238

CHAPTER ONE

Introduction

Overview

Behavioral health technicians (BHTs) are a key component of the U.S. military's behavioral health workforce. BHTs are enlisted service members who work alongside licensed mental health providers (MHPs), including psychiatrists, psychiatric nurse practitioners, psychologists, and social workers. Depending on their service branch, these personnel might be referred to as mental health technicians or behavioral health specialists, but we use the term *BHTs* in this report. In their clinical roles, BHTs serve as care extenders—members of the care team who provide supportive clinical services alongside licensed independent providers in the Military Health System (MHS). Ideally, care extenders support MHPs and improve the efficiency and effectiveness of behavioral health care. To ensure that BHTs are being integrated into clinical care in a way that makes the best use of their training and clinical skills, the MHS needed a better understanding of these service members' selection, training, roles and responsibilities, and supervision in clinical settings.

The U.S. Department of Defense's (DoD's) Psychological Health Center of Excellence (PHCoE) asked RAND to assess the current functional operation and utilization of BHTs in the MHS and to develop actionable recommendations to optimize their contributions in supporting the delivery of high-quality behavioral health care. The first phase of this research was a review of relevant curriculum, policies, and literature, with the goal of documenting the training, roles, and scope of practice of BHTs across service branches (Holliday et al., 2019). This report describes the findings from the second phase, a survey on the role of BHTs in the MHS, including perspectives of military BHTs and the MHPs with whom they work. These findings informed recommendations to standardize expectations regarding the role of BHTs in the MHS and to enhance the support they receive to maximize their contributions to the behavioral health and readiness of the force.

In this chapter, we provide a brief overview of the role of BHTs in the MHS; the results of our initial curriculum, policy, and literature review; and a rationale for examining how BHTs' roles can be optimized in the MHS.

Behavioral Health Technicians in the Military Health System

Enlisted personnel have been part of the military behavioral health workforce since the early 20th century (Harris and Berry, 2013). In the present day, BHTs complete technical training that prepares them to work alongside licensed MHPs in military treatment facilities (MTFs) or in embedded roles within units and in deployed settings. Their specific roles have evolved over time, but BHTs are currently trained to perform a variety of clinical support tasks, ranging from screening and assessment to assisting with psychotherapeutic interventions, treatment planning, and outreach activities (Air Education and Training Command Occupational Analysis Division, 2017; U.S. Air Force, 2015; U.S. Army Training and Doctrine Command, 2017; U.S. Army, 2017; U.S. Air Force, 2017; U.S. Navy, 2013). However, there have been concerns that BHTs are not being integrated in ways that maximize their training and skills. In part, this is due to competing demands (e.g., clinic administrative needs), but it is also unclear whether MHPs are aware of BHTs' skills or the best ways to integrate them into clinical settings (Holliday et al., 2019; Defense Health Board Task Force on Mental Health, 2007; Harris and Berry, 2013; Hoyt, 2018; Srinivasan and DiBenigno, 2016).

Curriculum, Policy, and Literature Review

In a prior phase of this study, we conducted a review of BHT training curriculum, relevant policies, and published literature (Holliday et al., 2019). In this section, we provide a brief overview of the findings of that review.

Our goal was to better clarify the selection, training, and roles and responsibilities of BHTs. In turn, this helped form the basis for our surveys of BHTs and MHPs, the results of which are presented in this report.

Our review of BHT curriculum included a site visit to the Medical Education and Training Campus (METC) located at Fort Sam Houston in San Antonio, Texas, where BHTs receive formal training. We reviewed METC curriculum and other relevant documents, including the Course Training Plan (Air Education and Training Command, 2015) and Resource Requirements Analysis Report (Health Care Interservice Training Office, 2015). We met with a small number of key informants, including METC administrators, instructors, and students, and observed students during practical components of their coursework (e.g., practicing patient assessments). We also reviewed military policies related to BHT training and practice, including those on METC training, scope of practice, supervisory expectations, and competency assessment. We supplemented this information with insights collected during discussions with BHTs and licensed MHPs from each service branch. Finally, we conducted a review of the published literature related to uniformed BHTs, along with the literature on civilian care extenders. The latter search was designed to identify any best practices, innovations, or frameworks that could inform MHS efforts to optimize the role of military BHTs. The following sections provide an overview of our findings, as well as updates drawn from literature published since that report was prepared.

Selection

The selection process for the BHT career field varies across service branches. For example, the Army requires that BHTs receive a certain score on the Armed Services Vocational Aptitude Battery skilled technical scale, have no criminal justice involvement, and meet physical qualifications (U.S. Army, undated; U.S. Army, 2017). BHTs in the Air Force must complete a personality assessment and participate in an entry interview conducted by a senior BHT or credentialed MHP (U.S. Air Force, undated; U.S. Air Force, 2015; U.S. Air Force, 2017). In the Navy, potential BHTs first train as hospital corpsmen through a 19-week curriculum before they are eligible to enter more-specialized behavioral health training (U.S. Navy Recruiting Command, undated; U.S. Department of the Navy, 2015; U.S. Navy, 2016).

Although the Army and the Air Force employ such tests as the Armed Services Vocational Aptitude Battery and Minnesota Multiphasic Personality Inventory–2 Restructured Form (MMPI-2-RF), respectively, the tests do not necessarily assess skills or characteristics that are specific to the BHT career (e.g., comfort with one-on-one contact with others, or ability to demonstrate empathy). In addition, none of the service branches explicitly assess student interest in the behavioral health field. Ideally, service members who embark on this career path have some interest in behavioral health. Yet due to documented shortages of BHTs in the past (U.S. Navy Personnel Command, 2018), it may likely be challenging to incorporate student interest as a formal selection criterion.

Training

Prior to entering the behavioral health workforce, BHTs participate in an intensive training course at METC, which includes a combination of didactic and hands-on components. The curriculum consists of three main elements: (1) a consolidated training component that is completed by students across service branches; (2) service-specific coursework, which covers topics that are specific to the roles that BHTs play in a given service branch; and (3) a clinical practicum. During the consolidated training component, BHTs complete eight courses over a period of nine and a half weeks. Topics covered in these courses range from ethics and psychopathology to more practical subject areas such as interviewing skills and psychological testing (Clay, 2016). BHTs then complete service branch–specific coursework covering topics relevant to the roles of BHT in each respective service branch (e.g., psychopharmacology, hospital medical systems) (Clay, 2016). At the conclusion of their formal training, BHTs engage in a directed clinical practicum that allows them to apply their newly acquired knowledge and skills in a clinical setting (Health Care Interservice Training Office, 2015). In partnership with ten military and civilian practicum sites, BHTs obtain exposure to a mix of inpatient and outpatient experiences as well as emergency rooms and psychological testing clinics (Holliday et al., 2019). The Army and the Navy require 203 hours of practicum training (or roughly five weeks), and the Air Force requires 96.5 hours (or about two weeks) of practicum training.

One of the main findings from our review of BHT training practices was that the volume of material covered in the curriculum makes it difficult to address significant topics necessary for clinical practice in much detail (Holliday et al., 2019). Though the curriculum aims to be comprehensive and cover a broad range of topics, it is unclear to what extent the curriculum reflects the work and experience that BHTs will encounter when in the workforce (e.g., the most common mental health diagnoses among active-duty service members). Our findings also indicated that the use of interactive and applied exercises to teach course material was limited, and BHTs have limited exposure to live demonstrations of clinical skills by their instructors prior to attempting the skill themselves. These practical and applied exercises are likely to be important for training mental health personnel (Beidas and Kendall, 2010; Holliday et al., 2019).

BHT Roles and Responsibilities

Our review of policy documents, job analyses, and competency rating forms indicated that BHTs are expected to take on a wide range of clinical, administrative, and unit responsibilities (Air Education and Training Command Occupational Analysis Division, 2017; U.S. Air Force, 2015; Headquarters, U.S. Department of the Army, 2017; U.S. Army Training and Doctrine Command, 2017; U.S. Navy, 2013). The roles and responsibilities of BHTs in garrison vary widely. BHTs are required to perform all clinical tasks under the supervision of a licensed MHP. Clinical responsibilities can often depend on the clinical setting as well as factors such as supervisor preferences and specific clinic demands. Some clinical responsibilities of BHTs include conducting initial intake assessments, triaging patients, participating in the administration of psychological screening instruments and tests, in addition to scoring such assessments. BHTs may also be relied upon to identify and communicate a patient's risk level and clinical needs to the licensed provider overseeing the case. Other clinical tasks that BHTs may be involved in include the provision of various psychosocial interventions, outreach and prevention services, and basic case management tasks, such as coordinating referrals for patients and developing treatment plans.

The amount of time spent on administrative duties can also vary by clinical setting and the availability of other administrative staff and the specific supervisor to which a BHT is assigned. BHTs may be tasked with answering phones, scheduling patients, records management, and coordinating handoffs for patients (Holliday et al., 2019). They might also be asked to fulfill some facility-level tasks, such as overseeing a prevention program or performing accreditation-related tasks. BHTs must also attend to certain unit and military responsibilities such as motor pool, overnight staff duty, and charge of quarters assignments (Hoyt, 2018). Studies have found that BHTs are being underutilized on clinical duties due to time spent on administrative tasks (Nielson, 2016; Defense Health Board Task Force on Mental Health, 2007). Therefore, some efforts have been implemented to ensure that BHTs achieve a certain number of client contact hours. Furthermore, Hoyt proposed a memorandum of understanding with a BHT's unit commander in order to formally establish expectations for military versus clinic duties for BHTs (Hoyt, 2018).

BHTs who deploy with medical and operational units may take on some of the same responsibilities as BHTs in garrison, but the role can differ significantly depending on the type of unit and branch of service. For example, BHTs in the Army might serve as part of Combat Operational Stress Control programs and be responsible for conducting intake and follow-up assessments, facilitating life skills classes, and potentially providing individual therapy, depending on the severity of a case (Potter et al., 2009; Smith-Forbes, Najera, and Hawkins, 2014). In the Air Force, BHTs might assist with preventive interventions at theater hospitals and expeditionary medical hospitals. In operational units, BHTs in the Army might serve as part of an embedded behavioral health team doing outreach and consultation (Holliday et al., 2019). Navy BHTs might serve as combat stress control professionals who are involved with activities such as leading psychoeducational classes and providing information on topics such as warning signs of stress-related topics (Holliday et al., 2019). BHTs in both the Army and Navy are also used to extend the reach of behavioral care across a greater geographic region, including with the use of telebehavioral health (Holliday et al., 2019).

As described, one key challenge is that BHTs are not consistently used to the full extent of their clinical training. Although it can be helpful for clinics to task BHTs with administrative tasks, this can limit BHTs' opportunities to practice, hone, and maintain clinical skills. Furthermore, it can have implications for BHTs who are deployed or assigned to operational settings, where BHTs might be responsible for providing services to work with a larger population and work more autonomously than BHTs in garrison.

In addition, there is an expectation that training at METC is only a foundation for BHTs' skills, and that OJT is required to continue to refine their skills. However, this involves a significant time investment by MHPs, who might not be well versed in the training needs of BHTs. For BHTs working in all different types of settings, there is limited guidance on specific expectations or requirements for supervision, ongoing training, and professional development. Together, these factors can further limit the roles and responsibilities of BHTs.

Supervision, Ongoing Training, and Professional Development

As noncredentialed providers (with the exception of certified alcohol and drug counselors [CADCs]), BHTs are required to work under the supervision of licensed MHPs, such as psychiatrists, clinical psychologists, licensed clinical social workers, and advanced-practice psychiatric nurses (Holliday et al., 2019). Depending on how a clinic is set up, a BHT might have one primary supervisor or receive oversight from multiple supervisors. Although there is limited information about the specific requirements for direct supervision, the Air Force outlines certain requirements for promotion within the BHT role, such as being trained and certified by a supervisor to perform a particular task (U.S. Air Force, 2015). Furthermore, there are currently efforts underway by some MTFs to create training programs for mental health providers, which includes a BHT supervision component (Holliday et al., 2019). Yet these types of programs, similar to policies around BHT supervision, are not standard across training sites and service branches.

There is also variation in the specificity of policies governing OJT and opportunities for ongoing professional development (e.g., service branch–funded courses, local and national conferences). OJT might entail having a supervisor sit in with a BHT as they meet with a patient, provide guidance during the appointment, and share feedback on the BHT's performance. Yet the extent to which this happens regularly, and in which contexts it takes place, is unclear. In addition, BHTs have varying types of continuing education. For example, Army BHTs are required to complete 12 hours annually of "accumulative study in the [behavioral health] field, either in a class, a self-study course or in-service training." However, these requirements are not based on a standard body of knowledge or competencies specifically designed for BHTs (Holliday et al., 2019). On the other hand, BHTs in the Air Force are expected to complete more standardized requirements, including career development courses (CDCs) and continuing education for recertification of their role as CADCs (Headquarters U.S. Air Force, 2019; U.S. Air Force, 2015). BHTs can also be ineligible to enroll in certain service branch–funded courses or attend local and national conferences with strict rank requirements (Holliday et al., 2019).

In turn, the limited guidance means that there may be uneven opportunities for BHTs to build their knowledge and skills. Our key informant discussions suggested that this has further implications for effectively integrating BHTs into clinical settings. For example, a mental health provider might expect BHTs to have a certain level of competency for particular tasks, but if those competencies have not been reinforced outside METC, they might not meet the expectations of the provider. Not only does this make MHPs more likely to simply assign administrative responsibilities to BHTs, but it also leaves BHTs less prepared for their next assignment, which can be particularly concerning in a deployed setting. Table 1.1 summarizes findings from our first report.

Recent Literature Regarding Behavioral Health Technician Training and Roles

Since our report was published, there has been some additional literature describing the roles and capabilities of BHTs.[1] A summary of findings from these publications is provided below.

One study conducted a job analysis of BHTs in embedded behavioral health roles within the Air Force (Ogle et al., 2019). Among the most common BHT tasks were spending time to develop rapport with unit members and leaders (e.g., through "walkabouts"), providing psychoeducation and health promotion programs, and providing consultation and advice to unit leadership. BHTs were less involved in operational tasks. Interpersonal

---

[1] We conducted a search to identify this new literature using a search terms adapted from our prior literature review, focusing on the following databases: Google Scholar, PsycInfo, ProQuest Military Database, Defense Technical Information Center, Congressional Research Service, National Academies Press, and PHCoE. Our search included any relevant literature that was released between December 2017 and May 2020. We then carried out a title and abstract review, which resulted in 16 additional documents.

TABLE 1.1

Summary of Key Challenges to the Effective Training and Use of BHTs

Domain	Key Challenges
Selection	• Selection processes risk selecting BHTs that may lack fit with the job.
Training	• The volume of material covered in the curriculum makes it challenging to cover topics essential to clinical practice in much detail. • Integration of interactive and applied exercises to teach course material can be variable across instructors.
BHT roles and responsibilities in garrison	• BHTs require OJT to develop their skills, but there appears to be no standard expectation for how OJT should be specifically operationalized, build in a meaningful way on METC training, and be widely disseminated and implemented in an effective and standardized manner. • BHTs are not consistently used to the full extent of their clinical training, and there is a need to better understand how factors such as the setting, supervisor preferences, and clinic administrative demands affect their roles to determine how they can be used more effectively.
Deployed and operational settings	• It is unclear whether and to what extent BHTs are prepared to fulfill the roles expected of them, especially in deployed or operational settings.
Supervision, ongoing training, and professional development	• There is limited guidance governing specific expectations or requirements for supervision, ongoing training, and professional development of BHTs.

SOURCE: Holliday et al., 2019.

skills, ability to practice effectively outside a traditional clinical setting, and skills in crisis assessment were among the top knowledge, skills, and abilities for BHTs in embedded positions. Of note, the authors recommended that BHTs have clinical experience before entering embedded behavioral health positions. As highlighted by a PHCoE blog post, BHTs may be particularly well suited to serving in embedded health roles because they have a shared culture with other members of the unit, and because enlisted service members may feel more comfortable approaching another enlisted individual rather than an MHP (Rehmert, 2020).

Another study demonstrated that BHTs can be trained to provide evidence-based psychotherapy (EBP) in deployed environments (Amin and

Wirtz, 2017). To increase access to cognitive behavioral therapy for insomnia, a protocol was developed that emphasized behavioral components of this intervention, an adaptation made to better match the training and skill level of BHTs. After a three-hour training, findings demonstrated that BHTs delivered the intervention with fidelity and patients experienced improvement in sleep. A recent PHCoE blog post also highlighted the potential role of BHTs in suicide prevention, including crisis intervention (e.g., through risk assessment and safety planning), outreach to military units, and through Combat Operational Stress Control interventions when in operational settings (Anthony, 2019).

Recent literature described some efforts to incorporate BHTs into the military's primary care–behavioral health integration efforts. For example, one quality improvement initiative teamed a BHT with an MHP in a primary care setting, allowing them to function as a behavioral health consultation team (Landoll et al., 2019). When a patient presented for a primary care behavioral health appointment, the BHT first engaged the patient by administering screening measures and conducting a functional assessment. The BHT then discussed the case with the MHP, who would meet briefly with the patient for treatment planning. This increased the average daily patient visits for the clinic, patients were satisfied with services received, and they were even more likely to recommend the clinic's integrated behavioral health services.

Recent literature has focused less on the supervision and training of BHTs. However, Krauss and Ballantyne (2019) described the role that BHTs play in doctoral psychology training programs. Specifically, they have developed a program at Fort Bragg that provides doctoral psychologist trainees with training on delivering clinical supervision to BHTs. Programs like this have the potential to benefit BHTs in multiple ways: Not only do they receive structured supervision, but the effort also ensures that a new generation of psychologists understand how to work with BHTs. An article focused on Army Reserve BHTs also discussed the establishment of a partnership with a civilian psychiatric emergency service to offer a training rotation, providing a mechanism of ensuring Reserve BHTs had sufficient opportunity to hone their skills in a clinical setting (Simpson, Goodwin, and Thurstone, 2019).

Together, these findings suggest that although there are some efforts to standardize and optimize the role of BHTs, many of the challenges outlined in our report remain.

Survey of Behavioral Health Technicians and Mental Health Providers

Our initial report offered four preliminary recommendations focused on establishing consistent selection criteria across service branches; approaches to creating a more targeted curriculum to maximize the applicability of material covered at METC; standardizing expectations for clinical roles, supervision, and ongoing professional development; and exploring whether there are existing models in the civilian sector that could be used to optimize the role of BHTs in the MHS. However, our ability to make concrete recommendations was limited by the lack of systematic data on the most common responsibilities and roles of BHTs across service branches. In addition, though our report highlighted that there may be concerns—on the part of both BHTs and MHPs—about the adequacy of BHT training, it is unclear how widespread these perceptions might be. Finally, our policy, curriculum, and literature review and key informant discussions raised some ideas as to current barriers to integrating BHTs into clinical settings and how the BHT role could be optimized. However, understanding the extent to which BHTs and MHPs agree with these perceived challenges and opportunities for optimizing their roles is key.

To address these unanswered questions and inform concrete recommendations for optimizing the role of BHTs, we developed two surveys: one for BHTs and one for MHPs. These surveys, designed to be largely parallel, aimed to obtain data on the treatment settings and current roles and responsibilities; perceptions of training; barriers to integrating BHTs into clinical settings; and perceptions of potential changes to BHT practice that might better capitalize on BHT skill and training. In turn, our aim was to describe current practice patterns, identify training needs, understand barriers and potential facilitators to integrating BHTs into clinical practice, and identify potential solutions.

Organization of This Report

This report provides an overview of the ways that BHTs are currently integrated into clinical care in the military and identifies opportunities to optimize their role. In Chapter Two, we describe our methods for administering a survey to BHTs and MHPs and our approach to data analysis. Chapters Three through Eight present our study findings. In Chapter Nine, we summarize our key findings and recommendations. Five appendixes include additional technical details on our survey sampling and weighting approaches (Appendix A), the domains and measures included in the surveys (Appendix B), the complete fielded BHT and MHP surveys (Appendixes C and D, respectively), and supplementary tables (Appendix E).

CHAPTER TWO

Methods

In this chapter, we describe the methods for understanding the scope of the BHT role across service branches, the nature and adequacy of training, perceptions of potential changes related to the BHT role both from the perspectives of BHTs and MHPs, and levels of satisfaction with the BHT role. All study methods were approved by RAND's Institutional Review Board, as well as by the Defense Health Agency Headquarters Human Research Protection Office. In addition, the survey was licensed by Washington Headquarters Services (DD-HA-2703) as an approved DoD internal information collection procedure.

Identifying Eligible Survey Participants and Sampling Strategies

Eligible Participants

With assistance from the Defense Manpower Data Center (DMDC), we identified eligible participants and drew two samples from the Health Manpower Personnel Data System: a sample of BHTs and a sample of MHPs. Eligible behavioral health technicians included active-duty service members from the Army (behavioral health specialists, 68X), Navy (behavioral health technicians, L24A), and Air Force (mental health technicians, 4C0X1). Eligible MHPs included licensed psychiatrists, mental health nurse practitioners, doctoral-level psychologists, and master's-level providers (i.e., social workers and master's-level psychologists). Both active-duty service members and DoD government civilians were eligible. Contractors were excluded from this study because their inclusion would have been subject to additional regulatory requirements. Finally, MHPs were required to have worked with a BHT in the previous 12 months to be eligible for participation. Because this information was not available in existing data, we used a screening item at the beginning of the survey to assess eligibility.

Sampling Strategy

We developed a sampling plan for each target population to provide the statistical power to support our analyses and ensure a representative sample of BHTs and MHPs. We selected two stratified, random samples with disproportionate allocation, or unequal probabilities. *Disproportionate allocation* refers to the practice of sampling certain substrata at higher rates than others. For instance, substrata with smaller populations might be sampled at higher rates than substrata with larger subpopulations. This process ensured that all subpopulations of interest were represented in our final sample and that planned comparisons were statistically powered. For BHTs, we stratified the sampling frame by service branch. For MHPs, we stratified the sampling frame by service branch, provider type, and military status. According to DMDC data, there were 2,236 eligible BHTs and 4,650 potentially eligible MHPs. MHPs were considered to be "potentially" eligible at the sampling stage because we needed to confirm eligibility using a screener item at the beginning of the survey, which asked whether they had worked with a BHT in the past year.

We relied on two primary sources to inform estimates of response rates and eligibility rates. First, we used detailed response rate information from a recent RAND survey of MHPs (Hepner et al., 2017). Second, we were informed by our recent report on BHTs, which described typical supervision arrangements for BHTs (Holliday et al., 2019).

Participation in a prior RAND survey of MHPs suggested that MHP response rates would vary by provider type and military status (i.e., active duty versus civilian). Specifically, we estimated response rates for active-duty MHPs would range from 33 percent (master's-level psychologists) to 52 percent (doctoral psychologists), as in our prior survey. Regardless of provider type, we estimated that active-duty providers would have a 10 percent higher response rate than civilian providers, which was similar to the marginal difference observed in the previous MHP survey. In addition, the previous MHP survey included an eligibility screening question to determine whether an MHP had actively provided psychiatric care to an adult patient with posttraumatic stress disorder (PTSD) or major depressive disorder at an MTF in the previous 30 days, finding that 78 percent of MHPs met this criterion. For the current survey, we used the eligibility rate from the prior survey as a proxy for estimating the proportion of MHPs who were likely to be currently working in clinical settings and would therefore have the opportunity to work with a BHT.

Because previous surveys of BHTs could not be used to inform their estimated response rates, we assumed a response rate of 40 percent for BHTs, which was similar to the overall response rate observed for MHPs. All active BHTs were eligible to participate in the survey, so estimated eligibility rates were not necessary for BHTs.

By combining the known population sizes of each sampling stratum with the estimated response rates and eligibility rates described above, we determined necessary sampling probabilities for each stratum to provide sufficient statistical power for planned comparisons across service branches and provider types. In total, we sampled 1,311 BHTs and 1,984 MHPs. Additional information about the sampling strategy is included in Appendix A.

Survey Development and Domains

The goal of the two surveys was to provide a clearer picture of the scope of BHT practice, from both BHTs' and MHPs' perspective. We developed largely parallel surveys to be fielded to BHTs and MHPs, which allowed us to explore these domains from both perspectives and develop a broader set of recommendations. Thus, the surveys covered the same six domains: demographic, service, and practice characteristics; clinical responsibilities and how those shift when deployed; perceptions of BHT training and supervision; barriers to integrating BHTs into clinical settings; BHT satisfaction with their duties and working environments; and perceptions of how BHTs could be more effectively integrated into the MHS. The BHT survey included 95 items, while the MHP survey included 88 items.

To develop the survey, we drew from existing, validated scales to the extent possible, grounded in a targeted review of the literature. Although we were able to draw a small number of items from existing surveys, many domains of interest required questions that were not available on other measures because our research questions were specific to the role of BHTs in the military context. Therefore, we developed many items based on the findings of our previous report. After developing survey drafts, we then completed an iterative review and revision process, obtaining input from RAND researchers, the Defense Health Agency's Behavioral Health Technician Work Group (BHTWG), and the Behavioral Health Clinical Community.[1]

Table 2.1 provides a summary of the survey domains and number of items on each domain. A more detailed description of the development of the survey and the content of each domain appears in Appendix B. The

TABLE 2.1

Survey Domains and Number of Items

Domain	Topics Assessed	Number of Items in BHT Survey	Number of Items in MHP Survey
Eligibility screen	Eligibility	0	1
Demographic, service, and practice characteristics	Sociodemographic characteristics, military experience, clinical settings, current roles, deployment experience	8	10
BHT responsibilities	Responsibilities, leadership status, deployment characteristics	56	47
Training and supervision	Training, provision, and receipt of supervision	6	6
Barriers to effective BHT practice	Perceptions of BHTs and their roles in the MHS	11	11
Satisfaction	BHTs' job satisfaction and MHP satisfaction with BHTs' performance	4	3
Perceptions of changes to BHT practice	Perceptions of potential policy, training, and role changes for BHTs	10	10
Total		95	88

---

[1] The Behavioral Health Clinical Community is a multidisciplinary group in the MHS that is working to improve behavioral health care through a variety of care-monitoring and process improvement activities.

complete BHT and MHP surveys are included in Appendixes C and D, respectively.

Survey Operations

To conduct the surveys, we partnered with Davis Research, a subcontractor with extensive experience in telephone and web-based survey administration. Given that surveys of health care providers often yield low response rates (Kellerman and Herold, 2001; VanGeest, Johnson, and Welch, 2008). RAND employed a mixed-mode strategy to increase the likelihood of achieving our intended response rates. With this strategy, participants had the option to complete the survey online or by telephone.

Due to limitations imposed by the Office of People Analytics (U.S. Department of Defense, 2015), we were limited to eight attempts to invite selected individuals to participate. This was a significant limitation, as surveys of those in the medical workforce may include eleven or more attempts (Parsons et al., 1994). Thus, our recruitment strategy depended on the available contact information for each respondent. There were three possible forms of contact information available: email address, telephone number (work or home), and home mailing address. Initial contact was always made via email (when available) or mailed letter (when email was not available). Email and letter invitations contained a link to an online survey, including a unique study code specific to the individual being invited to participate. Participants also had the option to complete the survey via telephone.

Most sampled individuals had all three forms of contact information (84.8 percent), and they received a combination of four emails, two mailed letters, and two telephone calls. Those who had only two forms of contact information receive a recruitment strategy customized to their available information.[2] Of the 3,029 participants with email addresses, less than 1 percent (0.4 percent) were not reachable (e.g., email bounced back or was

---

[2] Among those sampled, 7.6 percent had only a mailing address and telephone number and received a combination of three mailed letters and five telephone calls; 6.4 percent had an email address and mailing address only and received a combination of five emails and three telephone calls; and 0.2 percent had an email address and telephone number only and received a combination of four emails and four telephone calls.

no longer monitored); of the 3,273 with mailing addresses, 11.6 percent had bad or undeliverable addresses; and, of the 3,052 with telephone numbers, 7.8 percent were not reachable (e.g., number disconnected, fax machine/modem, wrong number).

The median survey completion time for the BHT survey was 44 minutes via phone and 20 minutes when participants took the survey online; for the MHP survey, it was 42 minutes via phone and 17 minutes online. Participants who completed the survey during off-duty hours received a $50 Amazon gift card. Survey respondents who completed the survey during their regular work hours were not eligible to receive an incentive because of DoD regulations.

To support survey participation, RAND aimed to publicize the survey and ensure eligible individuals were aware this survey was funded and supported by DoD. A RAND website, referred to in survey invitations, provided study information, contact information for key personnel, and a letter of support from the Defense Health Agency's BHTWG. In advance and during survey fielding, BHT and MHP leaders in each service branch were notified of the survey and encouraged to communicate support for the survey.

Response Rate

A total of 1,311 BHTs were invited to participate in the survey. Of those, 56.5 percent ($n = 742$) did not respond to the survey. Of the remaining 569 individuals, 15 individuals were not eligible because they were not currently working as active-duty BHTs and 4 did not consent to participate. The remaining 550 BHTs consented to participate in the survey, the majority of whom completed via web (70.5 percent). The raw response rate was 42.0 percent (550 participated out of 1,311 invited), but this rate does not account for the portion of the sample that we learned was ineligible after selection. Therefore, we computed an adjusted response rate that aligned with published guidelines (American Association for Public Opinion Research, undated). This rate effectively removed BHTs eventually deemed ineligible because they indicated before completing the survey that they were not currently active-duty BHTs ($n = 15$). This adjusted response rate was 42.4 percent (550 of 1,296).

A total of 1,984 MHPs were invited to participate in the survey. Of those, 59.3 percent (n = 1,177) did not respond to the survey. Of the remaining 807 individuals, 5.3 percent (105 MHPs) were not eligible because they reported they were not currently working with a BHT and 7 did not consent to participate. The remaining 695 completed at least one question in the survey, the majority of whom completed it via web (79.0 percent). The raw response rate was 35.0 percent (695 participated out of 1,984 invited), though this rate does not account for the portion of the sample we learned was ineligible after selection. We computed an adjusted response rate to remove MHPs deemed ineligible due to their response on the eligibility-screening item (n = 105) or inaccurate contact information (e.g., wrong mailing address for a respondent whose only form of contact information was a mailing address; n = 3). The adjusted response rate was 37.0 percent (695 of 1,876).

Data Analyses

Survey Weighting

We used statistical weighting to ensure that analyses reflected the relevant populations of interest. Weighted analyses were used to adjust for the disproportionate allocation we employed in our sampling design and the unequal response probabilities of different providers. Failing to incorporate sampling weights into downstream analyses may have resulted in biased conclusions.

The final weights included a design weight and a nonresponse weight. The design weight for each respondent was equal to the inverse of the probability of selection into each sample. The BHT sample was stratified only by service branch, so each BHT was assigned one of three design weights (corresponding to each service branch). Because the MHP sample was stratified by service branch, provider type, and military status, each MHP was assigned one of 30 design weights (corresponding to the 30 sampling strata derived from three service branches, five provider types, and two military statuses). To correct for nonresponse bias, which results when nonrespondents and respondents are systematically different, we computed a nonresponse weight for each respondent. This nonresponse weight was equal to the inverse of the probability of response of each individual. Whereas our sampling design weights were known, we needed to estimate the probability of each individual's response using statistical models. Specifically, we used a generalized boosted model that incorporated individual-level information on race, ethnicity, gender, paygrade, service branch, provider type, and military status (Griffin et al., 2014). The final weight was equal to the product of the design weight and the nonresponse weight. We provide further details of the weighting procedures, as well as a further discussion regarding limitations of this approach in Appendix A.

Final Analytic Sample

Of the 550 BHTs who responded to the survey, 12 individuals were removed because their survey responses indicated that they were not uniformed BHTs (e.g., they had recently separated from military) or were not currently working in the BHT career field. This resulted in a final analytic sample of 538 BHTs (Table 2.2). In addition, of the 695 MHP respondents, ten individuals were removed because their survey responses indicated that they were not an eligible provider type (e.g., nurse practitioner; $n = 4$) or were not currently working for the military as an MHP ($n = 6$). This resulted in a final analytic sample of 685 MHPs (Table 2.3).

Table 2.2 compares our final analytic sample of BHTs with the population of BHTs, and Table 2.3 does the same for MHPs. In both tables, the first two columns summarize the unweighted analytic samples while the second two columns summarize the population. We note that the unweighted sample proportions differed substantially from the corresponding population proportions. This is to be expected because certain substrata were deliberately oversampled to attain desired stratum-level sample sizes. For example, BHTs and MHPs serving in the Navy were overrepresented in our unweighted samples. Additionally, differential nonresponse between strata can cause the analytic sample to systematically differ from the population of interest. As discussed earlier in this chapter, we constructed survey weights to address both disproportionate sampling and nonresponse to ensure that estimates were representative of the populations of interest.

The rightmost column in Tables 2.2 and 2.3 illustrates the effect of the survey weights. We see that for both BHTs and MHPs, the characteristics of

TABLE 2.2

Final BHT Analytic Sample Compared with the BHT Population

Service Branch	Analytic Sample		Population		Analytic Sample % (weighted)
	n	% (unweighted)	*n*	%	
Army	194	36.1	1,148	51.3	50.9
Navy	103	19.1	231	10.3	10.6
Air Force	241	44.8	857	38.3	38.5

NOTE: *n* = 538.

TABLE 2.3

Final MHP Analytic Sample Compared with the MHP Population

Characteristic	Analytic Sample		Population		Analytic Sample % (weighted)
	n	% (unweighted)	*n*	%	
Provider type					
Psychiatrist	202	29.5	679	14.6	16.0
Psychiatric nurse practitioner	63	9.2	170	3.7	3.6
Psychologist (doctoral-level)	198	28.9	1,120	24.1	22.5
Psychologist (master's-level)	27	3.9	361	7.8	8.6
Social worker	195	28.5	2,320	49.9	49.4
Service branch					
Army	327	47.7	2,834	60.9	60.8
Navy	174	25.4	808	17.4	16.5
Air Force	184	26.9	1,008	21.7	22.8
Military status					
Active duty	407	59.4	1,941	41.7	46.4
Civilian	278	40.6	2,709	58.3	53.6

NOTES: The MHP population includes military and government civilian employee providers who may not be eligible to participate in the study. The population does not include contractor providers. Eligibility status could be determined only through a survey screener, so the population in this table includes some ineligible providers.

the weighted analytic sample closely follow the characteristics of the population (this can be seen by comparing the final two columns in each table). While the weighted sample is more similar to the population than is the unweighted sample, we note that the weighted proportions do not match the population proportions exactly. This occurs primarily because the population consists of both eligible and ineligible individuals, whereas the analytic sample consisted of eligible individuals only. If eligibility rates differed between substrata, then an analytic sample that is accurately weighted to reflect the eligible population may not match the characteristics of a population that contains both eligible and ineligible individuals. Because we do not know the eligibility status of nonrespondents, we cannot directly compare the demographics of the weighted analytic sample to the demographics of the eligible population. The discrepancies are more pronounced in the MHP sample (where the population and weighted proportions differ by as much as 4.7 percent) than they are in the BHT sample (where the population and weighted proportions differ by 0.4 percent at most). This is to be expected because the MHP population had a higher proportion of ineligible individuals than the BHT population. Further details can be found in Appendix A.

Analyses

We conducted descriptive analyses to examine survey-weighted percentages and means. We performed comparisons across service branch, time in training, and provider type (for MHPs only). To evaluate whether there were statistically significant differences across subpopulations of interest in all presented cross tabulations, we performed omnibus tests followed by post hoc pairwise comparisons when omnibus tests were significant at the $p < 0.05$ level. For continuous variables, omnibus tests were performed using survey-weighted generalized linear models. When responses were categorical, we performed survey-weighted chi-squared tests. Pairwise comparisons were performed using weighted two-sample t-tests (for numerical variables) and weighted chi-squared test (for categorical variables). We did not perform further adjustments to pairwise tests to account for multiple comparisons; performing unadjusted pairwise tests following significant omnibus tests has been shown to appropriately control the family-wise error rate (Carmer and Swanson, 1973).

In tables presenting cross-tabulated results, the significance of omnibus tests are presented using asterisks to denote standard levels of statistical significance (* $p < 0.05$, ** $p < 0.01$, *** $p < 0.001$). The results of pairwise comparisons are presented using Latin superscripts (i.e., *a*, *b*, and *c*). Pairs that are not significantly different share a common superscript, while pairs that do not share a common superscript are significantly different. A single group could contain multiple subscripts. For example, a group with the superscript *ab* is not significantly different from groups with the superscript *a* and not significantly different from groups with the superscript *b*. To protect the confidentiality of participants, in all cross-tabulated results, we suppress numerical findings in cells representing five or fewer respondents by replacing the data with *NR* (not reportable).

In addition to the cross tabulated results described here, we performed weighted Pearson correlation tests between pairs of numerical variables (e.g., BHT proficiency and BHT time in practice). Several analyses compared responses between the BHT and MHP populations across groups of analogous survey questions to understand concordance or discrepancies in perceptions and experiences. For example, we compared BHT and MHP responses regarding proficiency of 22 BHT tasks in Chapter Four. For these types of comparisons, we performed item-specific weighted two-sample *t*-tests. We also computed correlations of item means between BHTs and MHPs. For the group of proficiency questions, for example, we considered correlations between the vector of 22 BHT population means and 22 MHP population means. In these analyses, weighted means are computed, but unweighted correlation tests are performed.

In addition to these quantitative analyses, there was one open-ended question on the survey. To examine these responses, two members of the research team independently reviewed all responses to this question and inductively developed a set of codes to capture the major themes that were identified. All responses were then coded by both team members and discrepancies were discussed. During the process of resolving discrepancies, a small number of additional codes were identified. These codes were then applied by both team members and discussed to resolve discrepancies again.

Summary

This chapter summarized the survey methods, including sampling, survey development, survey administration, and data analysis. In the next chapter, we provide an overview of the demographic, service, and practice-related characteristics of the BHTs and MHPs who responded to our surveys.

CHAPTER THREE

Demographic, Service, and Practice Characteristics

In this chapter, we provide an overview of the characteristics of BHTs and MHPs who participated in the survey. We begin by describing demographic and service characteristics, including branch of service and military status, as well as time that BHTs and MHPs have been in practice. We then describe the current practice settings and roles of BHTs and MHPs, including the nature of BHTs' current assignments (e.g., whether in garrison or deployed) and the types of clinical settings in which BHTs and MHPs interacted with patients.

Demographic and Service Characteristics

As described, as part of our sampling plan, we selected a sample of BHTs representative of BHTs across the MHS with respect to branch of service, and a sample of MHPs representative with respect to branch of service, discipline, and military status (i.e., active duty or civilian). Survey respondents were weighted to reflect the characteristics of the overall populations of BHTs and MHPs.[1]

Demographic and military characteristics of BHTs and providers included in our analytic sample are presented in Table 3.1. At the time of the survey, about half of BHTs served in the Army (51 percent), 39 percent in the Air Force, and 11 percent in the Navy. Most respondents were either E-1–E-4 (47 percent) or E-5–E-6 (45 percent), with a smaller proportion of more senior BHTs responding to the survey (8 percent).

---

[1] Note that our sample of MHPs did not include contracted providers.

TABLE 3.1

Characteristics of BHTs and MHPs Included in the Analytic Sample

Provider Characteristics	BHTs (%) $n = 538$	MHPs (%) $n = 685$
Discipline (providers only)		
Psychiatrist	—	16.0
Psychiatric nurse practitioner	—	3.6
Doctoral-level psychologist	—	22.5
Master's-level psychologist	—	8.6
Social worker	—	49.4
Gender		
Female	45.5	61.4
Male	54.5	38.6
Race/ethnicity		
White	41.4	65.8
Black	19.8	13.4
Hispanic	23.1	11.0
Asian/Pacific Islander	9.1	4.4
Other	6.6	5.3
Service branch		
Army	50.9	60.8
Navy	10.6	16.5
Air Force	38.5	22.8
Military status		
Active duty	100.0	46.4
Civilian	0.0	53.6
Rank		
E-1 to E-4	47.0	—
E-5 to E-6	44.9	—
E-7 to E-9	8.1	—
O-1 to O-3	—	47.6
O-4 to O-6	—	52.4

NOTE: For MHPs, rank is reported for the subsample of active-duty respondents.

Among the MHPs, nearly half of respondents were social workers, followed by doctoral-level psychologists (23 percent) and psychiatrists (16 percent). About 61 percent of MHPs were from the Army, followed by Air Force (23 percent) and Navy (17 percent). MHPs were nearly evenly split between active-duty providers and DoD civilians.

A relatively small proportion of BHTs and MHPs reported that they had deployed in the previous 12 months (Figure 3.1). There were significant differences by service branch within BHTs. In Figure 3.1, the superscripts indicate which estimates were statistically different at the $p < 0.05$ level, according to post hoc paired comparisons. Estimates that share the same superscript (e.g., both labeled a) indicate comparisons that were not significantly different, whereas those with different superscripts (e.g., one labeled a and the other labeled b) are statistically different. Navy BHTs were significantly more likely to have recently deployed (33 percent), followed by Army (13 percent) and Air Force (5 percent). There were no significant differences across service branches for MHPs. Among the active-duty MHPs

FIGURE 3.1

BHT and MHP Recent Deployments, Overall and by Service Branch

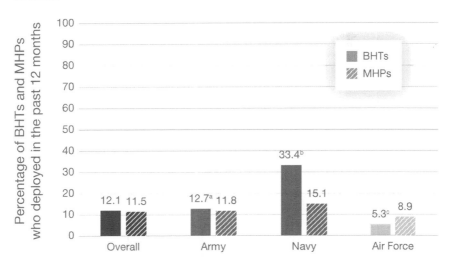

NOTES: Percentages of MHPs reflect active-duty MHPs only. Values with differing letter superscripts within a respondent type are statistically different at the $p < 0.05$ level, according to post hoc paired comparisons. BHTs: $n = 536$; MHPs: $n - 681$.

who deployed in the previous 12 months, most had worked with a BHT while deployed (82.6 percent).

On average, BHTs who responded to the survey had been in practice for about six years, but there was variability in the amount of experience across service branches (Table 3.2). BHTs in the Army had been in practice less time than their counterparts in the Navy and Air Force. For example, nearly a third of Army BHTs had been in practice less than two years (31 percent). By contrast, nearly all Navy respondents had been in practice for more than two years (99 percent). This variability in BHT experience across the service branches could have important implications for ongoing training and supervision needs.

Because MHPs include a mix of active-duty and DoD civilian providers, we examined both time in practice as an MHP and time in practice within the MHS. On average, MHPs had been in practice for 13.0 years (SD = 9.7). There were some significant differences across branch of service, with Army MHPs in practice longer (mean = 13.7, SD = 11.5) than Air Force MHPs (mean = 11.3, SD = 7.6) ($p < 0.05$). Navy MHPs fell between these two groups with respect to years of practice (mean = 12.4, SD = 7.5). The Air Force had a lower proportion of providers in practice more than 20 years (12.2 percent) compared to the Army (24.7 percent; $p < 0.05$). Of note, civilian providers reported significantly more years in practice (mean = 17.4, SD = 11.6) than active-duty providers (mean = 7.9, SD = 5.3; $p < 0.05$).

On average, MHPs had practiced in the MHS for 9 years, about four years less than the overall years of practice (Table 3.3). Most respondents

TABLE 3.2

BHT Time in Practice, Overall and by Service Branch

Time in Practice	Overall n = 538	Army n = 194	Navy n = 103	Air Force n = 241
Mean number of years in practice as a BHT (SD) ***	5.8 (4.6)	4.8 (4.7)[a]	7.0 (2.4)[b]	6.9 (4.9)[b]
0–2 years (%)	22.1	30.9	NR	16.2
2–7 years (%)	45.5	45.2	52.3	44.1
More than 7 years (%)	32.4	23.9	46.6	39.7

NOTES: * $p < 0.05$, ** $p < 0.01$, *** $p < 0.001$. NR = not reportable. Values with differing letter superscripts within rows are statistically different at the $p < 0.05$ level, according to post hoc paired comparisons. SD = standard deviation.

across branches had been practicing less than ten years in the MHS. There were no significant differences by service branch. Active-duty providers had significantly fewer years in practice in the MHS (mean = 7.6, SD = 5.0) than civilian providers (mean = 11.0, SD = 9.1; $p < 0.05$).

Differences in years of experience were also observed by provider type (Table 3.4) ($p < 0.01$). Psychiatrists and psychiatric nurse practitioners had an average of 10.4 years practicing as a mental health provider (SD = 6.7), whereas doctoral-level psychologists had been in practice an average of 13.1 (SD = 8.4) years, and master's-level clinicians had spent 13.9 (SD = 13.1) years

TABLE 3.3

MHP Time in Practice in the MHS, Overall and by Service Branch

Time in Practice	Overall n = 684	Army n = 327	Navy n = 173	Air Force n = 184
Mean number of years in practice in the MHS (SD)	9.4 (7.1)	9.5 (8.2)	10.0 (5.9)	8.9 (6.3)
0–5 years (%)	33.4	31.7	29.1	39.9
5–10 years (%)	30.2	31.6	33.8	24.9
10–20 years (%)	28.3	28.2	27.3	29.0
More than 20 years (%)	8.1	8.5	9.8	6.1

NOTES: * $p < 0.05$, ** $p < 0.01$, *** $p < 0.001$. Values with differing letter superscripts within rows are statistically different at the $p < 0.05$ level, according to post hoc paired comparisons.

TABLE 3.4

MHP Time in Practice in the MHS, by Provider Type

Time in Practice	Psychiatrist or Psychiatric Nurse Practitioner n = 262	Doctoral-Level Psychologist n = 211	Master's-Level Clinician n = 211
Mean number of years in practice in the MHS (SD)	8.9 (4.9)	10.0 (6.3)	9.4 (9.9)
0–5 years (%)	39.1	29.0	33.1
5–10 years (%)	28.7	31.6	30.5
10–20 years (%)	25.5	30.8	28.0
More than 20 years (%)	6.8	8.6	8.4

NOTES: * $p < 0.05$, ** $p < 0.01$, *** $p < 0.001$. Values with differing letter superscripts within rows are statistically different at the $p < 0.05$ level, according to post hoc paired comparisons.

in practice. However, there were no significant differences with respect to years of experience in the MHS, averaging about nine to ten years across provider types (Table 3.4).

Practice Settings and Roles

BHTs and MHPs reported on the settings in which they interacted with patients in the past month. For both BHTs and MHPs, outpatient mental health settings were most common (Figure 3.2). Outpatient substance use and integrated behavioral health settings were also common. Relatively few BHTs or MHPs reported interacting with patients in other clinical settings, including specialty care settings (e.g., inpatient substance use treatment settings) and medical care settings (e.g., primary care, emergency departments). Approximately half of BHTs (47.4 percent) and MHPs (54.2 percent) reported working in more than one treatment setting. Although this might expose BHTs to a broader range of clinical experiences, it might also make it more difficult for them spend the time needed to develop certain skills.

BHTs reported on other practice characteristics, including their current assignment and types of providers that they support. Regarding current assignment, we examined whether they were in garrison or deployed, and whether they were working in a medical setting or in an operational unit (Table 3.5). The majority of BHTs were in garrison MTFs (69 percent), followed by those in garrison operational units (16 percent). Only a small proportion of BHTs were in deployed settings (about 4 percent). There were some significant differences across service branch, with more Air Force BHTs currently in garrison MTF settings and more Army and Navy BHTs in garrison operational units (Table 3.5).

Nearly all BHTs reported that they support more than one type of provider (94.7 percent), and on average supported more than three types of providers (mean = 3.7, SD = 1.2). We did not ask explicitly whether these providers also serve as supervisors, but it is possible that BHTs receive some type of supervision from each MHP they support, even if just staffing cases with the MHP. This has the potential to make supervision and clinical oversight more complex (e.g., identifying a primary supervisor, responsibilities of MHPs with whom BHTs work). Regarding the types of

FIGURE 3.2
BHT and MHP Treatment Settings

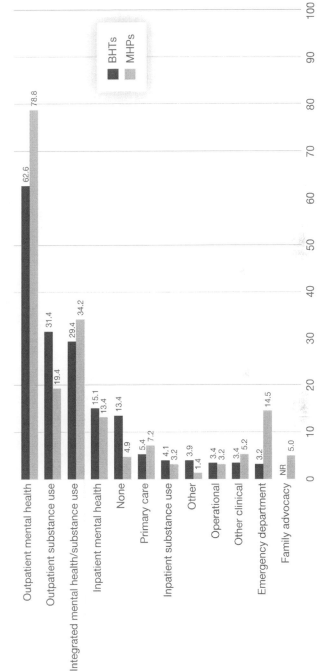

Percentage of MHPs and BHTs, by current treatment setting

NOTES: Treatment setting categories are not mutually exclusive. "Other" includes training, administrative, and assessment/selection settings. "Other clinical" includes telebehavioral health, forensic settings, and medical inpatient units. NR = not reportable. BHTs: *n* = 538; MHPs: *n* = 685.

TABLE 3.5

BHT Current Assignment, Overall and by Service Branch

Current Assignment	Overall (%) $n = 536$	Army (%)[a] $n = 194$	Navy (%)[a] $n = 103$	Air Force (%)[b] $n = 239$
In garrison MTF	69.3	57.7	57.0	88.2
In garrison operational unit	16.1	21.8	20.8	7.3
Deployed with a medical unit	2.3	3.3	5.4	NR
Deployed with an operational unit	1.4	NR	NR	NR
Nonclinical	6.2	7.7	7.9	3.6
Other	4.7	7.4	5.3	NR

NOTES: Because of the small cell sizes, statistical tests were performed on a collapsed version of the variable, with "deployed in a medical unit" and "deployed in an operational unit" combined and "nonclinical" and "other" combined. $* p < 0.05$, $** p < 0.01$, $*** p < 0.001$. NR = not reportable. Values with differing letter superscripts within rows are statistically different at the $p < 0.05$ level, according to post hoc paired comparisons. "Other" included unspecified garrison or deployed assignments.

MHPs they support in their current practice settings, BHTs most commonly reported supporting doctoral-level psychologists (93 percent), social workers (91 percent), and psychiatrists (81 percent) (Table 3.6). Fewer Army BHTs supported doctoral-level psychologists than Air Force BHTs; it was more common for Army BHTs to support master's-level psychologists than it was for those in the Navy or Air Force. Navy BHTs were less likely to support social workers than BHTs in the other service branches. To the extent that MHPs from different disciplines have different roles in clinical settings, this could result in differential skill development for BHTs (e.g., those supporting psychologists or social workers might have more exposure to counseling or psychotherapy).

We also assessed MHP practice characteristics, including supervision of BHTs and whether they serve in leadership roles in their clinics. Regarding supervision, though all MHPs worked with a BHT in the last year (as this was required to be eligible for the survey), less than half (43 percent) reported that they currently supervise a BHT (Figure 3.3). Differences across service branch were not statistically significant. Less than half (40 percent) of MHPs reported holding a leadership position in their clinic, such as being head of a clinic or clinical team. About half of Air Force and Navy MHPs held a lead-

TABLE 3.6

Providers Supported by BHTs, Overall and by Service Branch

Types of Providers Currently Supported	Overall (%) $n = 538$	Army (%) $n = 194$	Navy (%) $n = 103$	Air Force (%) $n = 241$
Psychiatrist	81.0	77.1	83.7	85.3
Psychiatric nurse practitioner	64.1	63.5	58.9	66.4
Doctoral-level psychologist**	93.2	89.8[a]	94.8[ab]	97.1[b]
Social worker***	91.3	92.0[a]	72.0[b]	95.8[a]
Master's-level psychologist***	32.9	43.4[a]	26.0[b]	21.2[b]
Drug and alcohol counselor[1]	1.9	NR	NR	NR
Nurse or case manager[1]	4.0	6.0	NR	2.3
Other	4.2	5.3	NR	2.7
None	1.2	NR	NR	NR

NOTES: Categories of providers supported are not mutually exclusive; respondents selected all that apply. * $p < 0.05$, ** $p < 0.01$, *** $p < 0.001$. NR = not reportable. Values with differing letter superscripts within rows are statistically different at the $p < 0.05$ level, according to post hoc paired comparisons. "Other" included occupational therapists, art/music therapists, and unspecified MHP trainees. There were uniformly low proportions of providers in the "Other" category, and expected cell sizes in corresponding contingency tables were not large enough to perform statistical significance tests.

ership role in clinic, compared to about one-third of Army MHPs. There was an association between holding a leadership position in one's clinic and currently supervising a BHT ($r = 0.27$, $p < 0.01$).

There were some differences observed by provider type, with psychiatrists or psychiatric nurse practitioners and doctoral-level psychologists more likely to supervise BHTs and hold leadership roles than master's-level clinicians (Figure 3.4). In turn, this has potential implications for understanding the capabilities of BHTs: MHPs who supervise BHTs are likely more familiar with their training and abilities, and those in leadership positions might have more input as to the role that BHTs play at a given clinic.

FIGURE 3.3

MHP Practice Attributes, Overall and by Service Branch

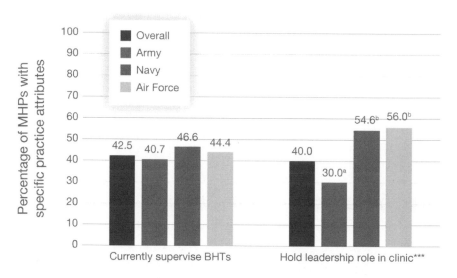

NOTES: $* p < 0.05$, $** p < 0.01$, $*** p < 0.001$. Values with differing letter superscripts within column clusters are statistically different at the $p < 0.05$ level, according to post hoc paired comparisons. MHPs who currently supervise BHTs: $n = 658$; MHPs who hold a leadership role in a clinic: $n = 680$.

Summary

This chapter provided an overview of the characteristics of BHTs and MHPs who participated in the survey, including demographic and service characteristics, as well as current practice settings and roles. Regarding BHTs, about half served in the Army, followed by Air Force and Navy. About two-thirds of MHPs also worked in the Army, followed by Air Force (23 percent) and Navy (17 percent). Nearly 60 percent of MHPs were master's level clinicians, including master's level counselors and social workers. On average, BHT respondents had spent about six years in practice as BHTs, though Navy BHTs had more years of experience. MHPs who participated in the survey had been practicing in the MHS for about nine years.

It was most common for BHTs and MHPs to be working in outpatient mental health and substance use treatment settings. Relatively fewer BHTs

FIGURE 3.4

MHP Practice Attributes, by Provider Type

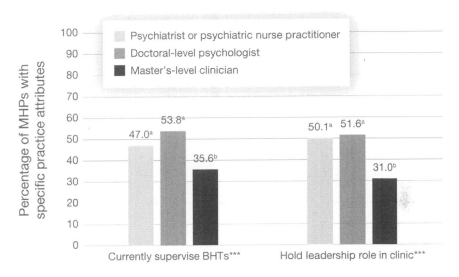

NOTES: * $p < 0.05$, ** $p < 0.01$, *** $p < 0.001$. Values with differing letter superscripts within column clusters are statistically different at the $p < 0.05$ level, according to post hoc paired comparisons. MHPs who currently supervise BHTs: $n = 658$; MHPs who hold a leadership role in a clinic: $n = 680$.

and MHPs were in other clinical settings or specialty programs (e.g., the Family Advocacy Program). About half of BHTs and MHPs reported interacting with patients across multiple settings. Nearly 70 percent of BHTs were assigned to in-garrison MTFs, with about 16 percent assigned to in-garrison operational units. Few BHTs were deployed at the time of the survey, and relatively few BHTs or MHPs reported having deployed in the previous 12 months. In turn, the type and number of settings in which BHTs work could influence the types of tasks they are asked to complete.

BHTs tended to work with multiple MHPs, and it was common for them to support psychiatrists, psychiatric nurse practitioners, doctoral-level psychologists, and social workers. However, a little less than half of the MHPs surveyed indicated that they currently supervise a BHT, although doctoral-level psychologists and prescribing providers were more likely to indicate that they did so.

CHAPTER FOUR

BHT Responsibilities and Clinical Tasks

In this chapter, we explore BHT roles and responsibilities from the perspectives of both BHTs and MHPs. This includes time spent conducting clinical tasks versus other types of responsibilities and the frequency with which BHTs complete a range of clinical tasks. We also explore the factors associated with the frequency of conducting clinical tasks.

Breakdown of BHT Responsibilities

BHTs reported on the percentage of time they spent in a typical week on each of four categories of activities. These included patient care–related clinical responsibilities, such as leading groups, conducting clinical interviews, or performing prevention activities; administrative clinic responsibilities, such as answering phones or making appointments; and nonclinical responsibilities, such as unit requirements and physical training. The fourth option was "other," for which respondents could note other activities that were in a typical week. Other activities that were reported included supervision, training, and management responsibilities. Respondents were asked to ensure that percentages of time they assigned to each type of activity summed to 100 percent.

BHTs reported engaging in an eclectic mix of activities in a typical week, with the proportion of time spent on each type of activity varying by service branch. Overall, BHTs indicated that they spent about one-third of their time in a typical week on administrative clinic responsibilities and one-third on patient care–related clinical responsibilities, followed by nonclinical responsibilities and other activities (Figure 4.1). The amount of time BHTs spent on these tasks differed significantly by service branch ($p < 0.05$). For instance, BHTs in the Air Force reported spending less time on patient care–related clinical responsibilities (26.4 percent) than their Army and Navy counterparts (35.4 percent and 35.8 percent, respectively). Army BHTs spent more time attending to nonclinical responsibilities (26.0 percent), such as unit requirements, compared with Navy (19.0 percent) and Air Force BHTs (20.9 percent).

We also examined whether time spent on patient care responsibilities varied according to the amount of time BHTs had been in practice, their current assignment,[1] or whether they had deployed in the past 12 months. BHTs who had been in practice longer spent significantly less time on patient care activities ($r = -0.32$, $p < 0.01$), which may reflect that more ten-

FIGURE 4.1

Percentage of Time BHTs Spent on Activities in a Typical Week

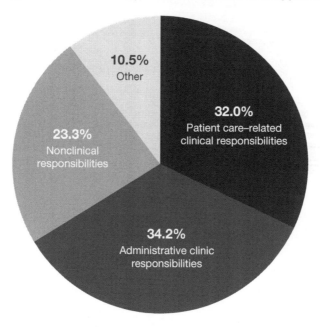

NOTES: "Other" includes supervision, training, and management responsibilities. BHTs: $n = 497$.

---

[1] This analysis used a collapsed version of the variable reported in Chapter Three. The collapsed version focused on whether the assignment was in garrison at an MTF, a garrison operational unit, deployed setting, or other setting.

ured BHTs are more likely to get tasked with additional leadership responsibilities (e.g., MTF responsibilities, unit responsibilities). There was no significant association between time spent on patient care responsibilities and current assignment or recent deployment history.

Frequency of BHT Clinical Tasks

To better understand BHTs' clinical responsibilities, BHTs were asked how frequently they currently performed each of 22 tasks on a five-point scale ranging from never to very often. These tasks covered four categories: screening/assessment (e.g., triage walk-in patients, administer and score behavioral health symptom measures); psychosocial interventions (e.g., provide supportive counseling for mental health concerns; facilitate group counseling or group therapy sessions); treatment planning/ monitoring (e.g., develop treatment plans, review patient homework or logs); and outreach/resilience (e.g., conduct behavioral health outreach to units or base community to provide information about behavioral health services, provide behavioral health consultation in non–behavioral health clinical settings). In this section, we describe the frequency with which BHTs perform each of the 22 tasks. We then examine the variation in frequencies by BHTs' service branch, current assignment, and deployment status to identify factors that might contribute to differences in the frequency with which BHTs perform specific tasks.

BHT-Reported Frequency of Tasks

First, we examined the frequency that BHTs reported conducting each of the 22 tasks. Figure 4.2 shows each task, ordered by the frequency that BHTs endorsed conducting the task (either often or very often). The most common task was conducting risk assessments, with nearly three quarters of BHTs (73 percent) reporting that they conduct risk assessments often or very often. Roughly half of BHTs indicated that they use the Behavioral Health Data Portal (51 percent), a web-based platform designed to facilitate routine symptom assessments, often or very often. Further, about half of BHTs reported they often or very often conduct intake interviews (49 percent) and administer and score behavioral health symptom measures (49 percent). In

FIGURE 4.2

Percentage of BHTs Who Reported Performing Tasks Often or Very Often

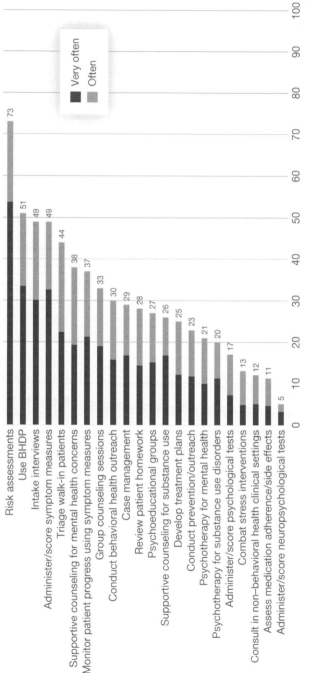

NOTE: *n* = 527–530.

addition, about 43 percent of BHTs noted that they often or very often triage walk-in patients.

We also examined the frequency with which BHTs said they "never" perform each task. We provide an overview of findings here, and complete results can be found in Appendix E. There were some tasks that a substantial proportion of BHTs indicated that they never perform, including administering and scoring cognitive and neuropsychological tests (61 percent never performed this task) and providing behavioral health consultation in non–behavioral health clinical settings (54 percent). Other tasks that were infrequently performed included assessing medication adherence and side effects (51 percent), delivering specific EBPs for substance use disorders (47 percent), and conducting combat stress briefings, trainings, or interventions (43 percent).

Variation in BHT Tasks by Service Branch

In this section, we examine variation in the frequency with which BHTs in each service branch perform specific types of tasks. To reduce the number of comparisons required, we grouped the 22 tasks into four subscores: screening/assessment, psychosocial interventions, treatment planning/monitoring, and outreach/resilience. Item assignment to subscores can be found in Table B.2 in Appendix B. For each subscore, we computed an average (i.e., mean of available items). Scores ranged from 0 (never) to 4 (very often). We examined the psychometric properties of these subscores. Internal consistency reliability (Cronbach's alpha) ranged from 0.82 (outreach/resilience) to 0.86 (psychosocial intervention, treatment planning/monitoring), suggesting that items grouped within each subscore were highly related to each other. Correlations between subscores ranged from 0.47 (between psychosocial interventions and outreach/resilience) and 0.78 (between psychosocial intervention and treatment planning/monitoring). We note that we did not conduct formal scale development; thus, these analyses are aimed at highlighting potential patterns in variations in practice.

BHTs reported that they most frequently perform screening/assessment tasks, followed by psychosocial interventions, treatment planning/monitoring, and outreach/resilience tasks (Table 4.1). Reported frequency of tasks differed significantly by branch of service. For example, Air Force BHTs reported performing screening/assessment tasks and treatment planning/

41

TABLE 4.1

BHT-Reported Frequency of Tasks, Overall and by Service Branch

Subscore	Mean (SD)			
	Overall	Army	Navy	Air Force
Screening/assessment***	2.0 (1.0)	1.8 (1.2)[a]	1.9 (0.6)[a]	2.2 (0.8)[b]
Psychosocial interventions***	1.6 (1.1)	1.4 (1.3)[a]	1.7 (0.7)[b]	1.8 (1.0)[b]
Treatment planning/ monitoring***	1.5 (1.1)	1.1 (1.1)[a]	1.6 (0.8)[b]	1.9 (1.1)[c]
Outreach/resilience**	1.3 (1.0)	1.2 (1.3)[a]	1.4 (0.8)[ab]	1.5 (0.9)[b]

NOTES: ** $p < 0.01$, *** $p < 0.001$. Values with differing letter superscripts within rows are statistically different at the $p < 0.05$ level, according to post hoc paired comparisons. Overall: $n = 527$–530; Army: $n = 187$–189; Navy: $n = 102$–103; Air Force: $n = 238$.

monitoring tasks more often than Army and Navy BHTs. Army BHTs reported performing psychosocial interventions and treatment planning/ monitoring activities significantly less than Navy and Air Force BHTs.

Variation in BHT Tasks by Current Assignment

Next, we examined whether there were differences in the amount of time BHTs spent on certain types of tasks, depending on their current assignment. Current assignments include serving in garrison MTFs, garrison operational units, deployed settings, and other clinical and nonclinical settings. We analyzed the four task subscores (i.e., screening/assessment psychosocial interventions, treatment planning/monitoring, and outreach/ resilience) to explore if the frequency with which BHTs performed different tasks varied across these assignments.

BHTs reported performing screening/assessment tasks, psychosocial interventions, and treatment planning/monitoring tasks most frequently in garrison MTF settings ($p < 0.05$). The frequency of outreach/resilience tasks was similar across settings. Screening and assessment activities were performed most often across all assignment settings, as indicated by the mean frequency score (mean = 2.0). Our prior findings (Holliday et al., 2019) suggested that BHTs who were currently deployed may be engaging in certain tasks more frequently. This might be due to the nature of the setting (e.g., outreach and resilience tasks may be more common in deployed settings) or due to the reduced behavioral health workforce (i.e., with fewer MHPs and BHTs, BHTs might engage in clinical activities more often than in garrison settings). However, this does not appear to be the case.

Association Between Frequency of Tasks and Practice Attributes

We hypothesized that there might be a relationship between how often BHTs perform certain types of tasks and the amount of time that they have been practicing as a BHT, which may indicate whether more experienced BHTs tend to perform certain types of tasks at a different frequency compared with newer BHTs. In addition, we hypothesized that there might be an association between the amount of time BHTs spend performing patient care activities and the frequency with which BHTs perform particular tasks.

In order to assess this, we examined the correlation between frequency of tasks and the time in practice as a BHT, as well as time spent performing patient care activities (Table 4.2). There was a small negative correlation between frequency of screening/assessment activities and BHT time in practice, suggesting that BHTs with less practice experience spend more time in screening/assessment tasks. This may reflect the fact that BHT technical training has a strong focus on screening, intakes, and triaging patients, and that these skills may require less additional OJT than such tasks as psychosocial interventions or treatment planning. In addition, BHTs who had been in practice longer reported more frequent involvement in outreach/

TABLE 4.2

Association Between BHT-Reported Frequency of Tasks and Practice Attributes

Subscore	BHT Time in Practice (correlation)	BHT Time Spent on Patient Care Activities (correlation)
Screening/assessment	−0.20***	0.45***
Psychosocial interventions	0.02	0.44***
Treatment planning/ monitoring	0.06	0.28***
Outreach/resilience	0.15**	0.14**

NOTES: ** $p < 0.01$, *** $p < 0.001$. Screening/assessment: $n = 530$; psychosocial interventions: $n = 530$; treatment planning/monitoring: $n = 529$; outreach/resilience: $n = 527$.

resilience tasks. Significant associations were observed between BHT time in patient care activities and each subscore, with the highest correlations observed for screening/assessment activities ($r = 0.45$) and psychosocial interventions ($r = 0.44$).

Summary

This section examined BHTs' reported frequency for performing various types of tasks. We found that BHTs across all service branches reported performing screening and assessment tasks most often, and outreach and resilience activities least often. In addition, BHTs reported performing screening/assessment, psychosocial interventions, and treatment planning/monitoring activities most frequently in garrison MTFs. Finally, we also observed some significant associations between BHTs' time in practice and how often they performed certain tasks.

MHP-Reported Frequency of Tasks

MHPs were also asked to report on the frequency with which the BHTs they worked with currently perform each of the same 22 tasks. Figure 4.3 summarizes the tasks that MHPs reported that the BHTs they work with perform often or very often. Almost 60 percent of MHPs reported that they observe BHTs using the Behavioral Health Data Portal and triaging walk-in patients often or very often, followed by conducting risk assessments (53 percent). Other screening/assessment tasks were also commonly endorsed, including administering and scoring behavioral health symptom measures (52 percent) and conducting intake interviews (47 percent).

We also examined the tasks that MHPs indicated that BHTs "never" perform (Figure E.2 in Appendix E). Nearly three-quarters of MHPs reported that BHTs never administer and score cognitive and neuropsychological tests (73.4 percent). About two-thirds of MHPs indicated that BHTs never provided behavioral health consultation in non–behavioral health clinical settings (63.2 percent) or assessed medication adherence and side effects (60.4 percent).

Variation in BHT Tasks by Service Branch

This section further explores MHPs' perceptions regarding the frequency with which BHTs in each service branch perform certain types of tasks.

FIGURE 4.3

Percentage of MHPs Who Reported That BHTs Performed Tasks Often or Very Often

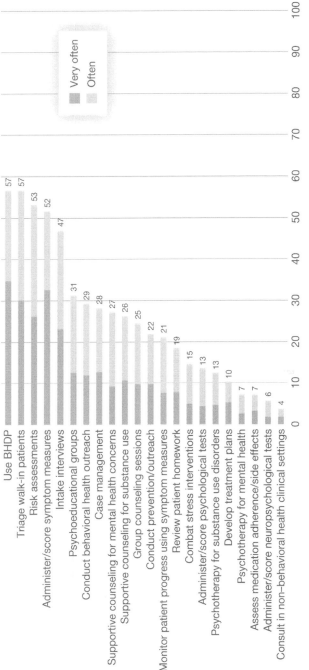

Percentage of MHPs reporting that BHTs performed tasks often or very often

NOTES: *n* = 651–659. BHDP = Behavioral Health Data Portal.

Similar to analyses focused on BHT-reported frequency of tasks, we computed four subscores reflecting the MHP-reported frequency screening/assessment, psychosocial interventions, treatment planning/monitoring, and outreach/resilience tasks. Internal consistency reliability (Cronbach's alpha) for the subscores ranged from 0.77 (screening/assessment) to 0.83 (psychosocial intervention, outreach/resilience). Correlations between subscores ranged from 0.47 (between screening/assessment and outreach/resilience) and 0.72 (between psychosocial intervention and treatment planning/monitoring).

MHPs reported screening/assessment activities as the most frequent types of tasks performed by BHTs (Table 4.3), followed by psychosocial interventions, outreach/resilience tasks, and treatment planning and monitoring tasks. MHP perceptions of the frequency of BHT tasks differed significantly across service branches (Table 4.3). MHPs in the Air Force reported that BHTs performed each type of task more frequently in comparison with MHPs in the Navy and Army.

Variation in BHT Tasks by Provider Type and Supervisor Status

In this section, we examine variation in the frequency with which MHPs observed BHTs performing certain tasks by MHPs' discipline and whether they supervised BHTs. These factors could shape the interactions MHPs have with BHTs, as well as the tasks that get assigned to BHTs.

TABLE 4.3

MHP-Reported Frequency of Tasks, Overall and by Service Branch

Subscore	Mean (SD)			
	Overall	Army	Navy	Air Force
Screening/assessment***	2.0 (0.8)	1.9 (0.9)[a]	1.9 (0.6)[a]	2.3 (0.7)[b]
Psychosocial interventions***	1.3 (0.9)	1.1 (1.0)[a]	1.3 (0.7)[a]	1.9 (0.8)[b]
Treatment planning/ monitoring***	1.1 (1.0)	0.9 (1.0)[a]	1.2 (0.7)[b]	1.7 (1.0)[c]
Outreach/resilience***	1.2 (1.0)	0.9 (1.0)[a]	1.1 (0.8)[a]	1.9 (0.9)[b]

NOTES: *** $p < 0.001$. Values with differing letter superscripts within rows are statistically different at the $p < 0.05$ level, according to post hoc paired comparisons. Overall: $n = 651$–669; Army: $n = 314$–319; Navy: $n = 168$–172; Air Force: $n = 179$–180.

We examined whether perceived frequency of BHT tasks varied by the discipline or whether the MHP reported supervising a BHT. Doctoral-level psychologists tended to report that BHTs performed psychosocial interventions and treatment planning/monitoring tasks less often than master's-level clinicians and psychiatrists or psychiatric nurse practitioners ($p < 0.05$). Of interest, MHPs who reported supervising BHTs endorsed a higher frequency of task performance for all subscores than those who did not supervise BHTs ($p < 0.05$). This might reflect a greater awareness of BHTs' activities on the part of MHPs who supervise BHTs. With regard to the military status of MHPs, we found that active-duty MHPs observed BHTs completing tasks across all subscores to a greater extent than their civilian counterparts ($p < 0.05$).

Variation in BHT Tasks by Military Status and Deployment History

Furthermore, we examined the variation in MHPs' reported frequency of tasks by their military status and deployment history. This analysis allows us to better understand how military-related experiences might be associated with MHPs' perspectives on the frequency of BHT tasks.

MHPs who reported supervising BHTs endorsed a higher frequency of task performance for all subscores than those who did not supervise BHTs ($p < 0.05$). This might reflect a greater awareness of BHTs' activities on the part of MHPs who supervise BHTs. There were no differences in the reported frequency of BHT tasks among MHPs who had been deployed with a BHT in the previous 12 months compared with those who had not. As noted earlier, our previous findings suggested a difference in the tasks that BHTs perform while deployed. However, these findings indicate that there was little variation in frequency of certain tasks observed by MHPs regardless of deployment history. With regard to the military status of MHPs, we found that active-duty MHPs observed BHTs completing tasks across all subscores to a greater extent than their civilian counterparts ($p < 0.05$).

Summary

This section examined the frequency with which MHPs reported observing BHTs perform certain types of tasks. Through our analysis, we found meaningful differences according to MHPs' service branch, provider type, military status, and supervisor status. On the other hand, there were no significant differences in reported frequency of tasks by MHPs who had worked with BHTs while deployed in the previous 12 months compared with those who had not.

Concordance Between BHT- and MHP-Reported Frequency

To further understand the extent to which BHTs and MHPs responded similarly about how often BHTs perform each of the 22 tasks, we conducted two analyses. First, to examine concordance between BHT- and MHP-reported frequency of tasks, we computed the correlation between BHT and MHP responses. Second, we were interested in whether there were discrepancies between the reports of BHTs and MHPs. To examine this, we performed a descriptive comparison of the percentage of BHTs and MHPs who reported that each task was completed often or very often. We also calculated whether there were significant differences in the mean frequency of each task as reported by BHTs and MHPs, using the subscores computed for analyses above.

Regarding the concordance between BHT and MHP responses, there was a large, significant correlation between mean BHT item scores and MHP item scores ($r = 0.91$) across the 22 items. This indicates that BHTs and MHPs were largely in agreement about the types of tasks that BHTs more frequently complete ($p < 0.001$). We also examined correlations between BHT-reported and MHP-reported frequency of tasks by service branch. These correlations ranged from 0.80 for the Air Force to 0.93 for the Army ($p < 0.01$), suggesting high agreement within service branches.

Although there was an association between BHT and MHP responses, our descriptive analyses suggested that BHTs reported completing tasks more often than MHPs observe. For example, conducting risk assessments was a highly endorsed task by both BHTs and MHPs. However, about 73 percent of BHTs reported performing this task often or very often, compared with the 53 percent of MHPs who reported that BHTs they work with conducted risk assessments often or very often. We identified the top five tasks with the highest discrepancy in the percentage of respondents indicating that BHTs completed the task often or very often (Figure 4.4). Discrepancies

FIGURE 4.4

Top Five Discrepancies Between BHT-Reported and MHP-Reported Frequency with Which BHTs Performed Tasks

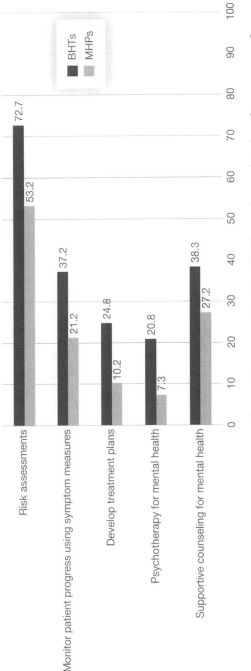

Percentage reporting that BHTs performed tasks often or very often

NOTES: BHTs: *n* = 528–530; MHPs: *n* = 661–665.

were observed both for fairly common tasks (e.g., risk assessment) and for less common tasks (e.g., EBP for mental health concerns). The highest discrepancy was observed for risk assessment (19.4 percent difference between BHT and MHP ratings).

Regarding differences in the mean frequency of tasks, BHTs reported that they completed psychosocial intervention and treatment planning/ monitoring tasks significantly more often than perceived by MHPs ($p < 0.001$). However, there was no significant difference in the subscore scores for screening tasks or outreach/resilience tasks. In addition, we computed t-tests to determine whether there were any significant differences in the frequency with which BHTs in each service branch performed each type of task. Although there were some significant differences across service branches, there were no clear patterns (analysis not shown).

Summary

This chapter provided information about the frequency of tasks that BHTs perform as reported by both BHTs and MHPs. Results indicated that, in a typical week, BHTs spend about one-third of their time in patient care activities—but also an equivalent amount of time on administrative clinic responsibilities. They spent nearly one-quarter of their time on nonclinical responsibilities. Previous research has suggested that BHTs may not spend a substantial portion of their duty hours on clinical tasks, given other competing demands (Nielson, 2016), and our results support that conclusion. In turn, the limited time spent on patient care activities can have important implications for skill development, especially given the role of OJT in BHT training. It also has implications for deployment, during which time BHTs spend more time on certain types of tasks, including screening/assessment, psychosocial interventions, and outreach/resilience.

According to BHTs and MHPs who participated in our surveys, BHTs' most common tasks are conducting risk assessments, using the Behavioral Health Data Portal, conducting intake interviews, administering and scoring behavioral health symptom measures, and triaging patients—all screening- and assessment-related activities. By contrast, not many BHTs engaged in neuropsychological or cognitive testing, consultation in non–

behavioral health settings, or assessing medication adherence or side effects. Our findings suggest that Air Force BHTs were most engaged in clinical tasks across categories; their mean frequency ratings were higher than those of BHTs in the other service branches. This might reflect the well-defined career progression standards and the detailed policy documents outlining the expected roles of BHTs in the Air Force (U.S. Air Force, 2015, 2017). In Chapter Five, we discuss BHTs' and MHPs' perceptions of BHT proficiency in performing these tasks.

CHAPTER FIVE

Perceptions of BHT Proficiency

In this chapter, we discuss BHTs' and MHPs' perceptions of BHTs' proficiency of their role and responsibilities. Specifically, we consider BHTs' self-reported proficiency in completing various clinical tasks, and MHPs' perceptions of BHTs' competence to complete those same tasks. We also explore perceptions of BHTs' skill level for those tasks. In addition, we examine the relationship between BHTs' and MHPs' reported levels of BHT proficiency. Finally, we discuss changes to practice patterns while BHTs are in deployed settings and tasks that BHTs and MHPs perceive to be out of scope.

BHT and MHP Perceptions of BHT Proficiency

In addition to reporting the frequency with which they perform clinical tasks, we asked BHTs to report their level of confidence for performing each task. Responses were reported on a four-point scale, which included "I cannot perform this task," "I can perform this task with assistance," "I can perform this task with no assistance," and "I can perform this task with no assistance and I can train someone to perform this task." We refer to this as *BHT-reported proficiency*. Second, we asked MHPs to indicate the level at which they believe BHTs are proficient at performing the same set of 22 tasks ("MHP-reported proficiency"). Response options ranged from "They cannot perform this task" to "They can perform this task with no assistance and they can train someone to perform this task."

In this section, we describe BHT-reported proficiency across clinical tasks and whether these perceptions vary by service branch. We also examine whether there is an association between BHTs' self-reported level of proficiency and two practice attributes: (1) time in practice and (2) time in patient care activities. We then examine MHPs' perspectives on BHT proficiency on certain tasks and variation in MHPs' perspectives according to five MHP characteristics: service branch, provider type, military status, supervisor status, and deployment history. Finally, we compute the correlation between MHP-reported proficiency and MHPs' time in practice, as well as their time practicing within the MHS.

BHT-Reported Proficiency in Performing Clinical Tasks

Figure 5.1 summarizes the percentage of BHTs who reported that they can perform a task with no assistance *or* perform a task with no assistance and train others on the task. The majority of BHTs reported being proficient in conducting risk assessments (97 percent), triaging walk-in patients (96 percent), and conducting intake interviews (94 percent). BHTs were also confident in using the Behavioral Health Data Portal (84 percent) and administering and scoring symptom measures (83 percent). Perhaps not surprisingly, these are among the tasks that most BHTs reported performing frequently.

In an effort to identify the tasks that BHTs feel less proficient performing, we also examined the proportion of BHTs who responded, "I cannot perform this task" for each task (Figure E.3 in Appendix E). About one third of BHTs indicated that they could not assess medication adherence and side effects (30.6 percent) or administer and score cognitive and neuropsychological tests (30.4 percent). Substantial proportions of BHTs also reported that they cannot perform specific evidence-based practices for substance use disorders (28.7 percent), deliver specific evidence-based practices for mental health (22.5 percent), or provide behavioral health consultation in non–behavioral health clinical settings (21.2 percent). These are all tasks that BHTs reported performing less frequently, which could indicate that BHTs feel more comfortable with tasks they conduct more often but might also indicate that they avoid tasks that they feel they are less proficient in performing.

Variation in BHT Self-Reported Proficiency by Service Branch, Current Assignment, and Deployment History

We hypothesized that a number of factors could influence BHTs' ratings of their proficiency, including their service branch, current assignment, or

FIGURE 5.1

Percentage of BHTs Who Reported Ability to Perform a Task with No Assistance and to Train Someone Else on That Task

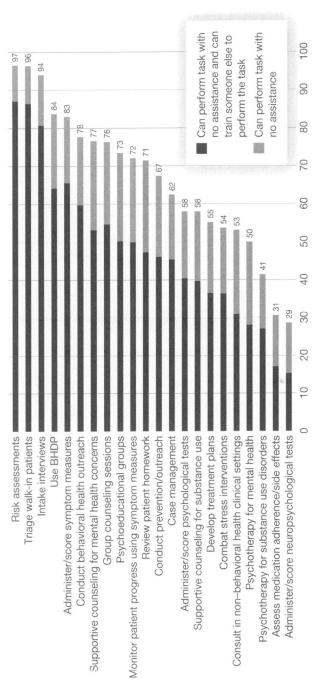

NOTE: *n* = 517–527.

whether they recently deployed. In this section, we explore the variation in the extent to which BHTs perceive themselves to be proficient at various tasks across service branches.

To examine the factors that contribute to the BHT-reported proficiency for performing various tasks, we created four subscores reflecting the average ratings of BHT-reported proficiency for each category of tasks (screening/assessment, psychosocial interventions, treatment planning/monitoring, and outreach/resilience). Item assignment to subscores are provided in Table B.2 in Appendix B. Scores ranged from 0 ("I cannot perform this task") to 3 ("I can perform this task with no assistance and I can train someone to perform this task"). Internal consistency reliability (Cronbach's alpha) ranged from 0.77 (screening/assessment) to 0.86 (psychosocial intervention). Correlations between subscores ranged from 0.48 (between screening/assessment and psychosocial interventions) and 0.77 (between psychosocial intervention and treatment planning/monitoring).

As shown in Table 5.1, BHTs across all service branches reported being most proficient in screening/assessment tasks, but we observed significant differences across service branches. Compared to Army and Navy BHTs, Air Force BHTs reported significantly higher proficiency in screening/assessment, treatment planning/monitoring, and outreach/resilience tasks. Although there was some variation in self-reported proficiency ratings among BHTs, depending on their current assignment, few clear trends were

TABLE 5.1
BHT-Reported Proficiency in Performing Tasks, Overall and by Service Branch

	Mean (SD)			
Subscore	Overall	Army	Navy	Air Force
Screening/assessment***	2.3 (0.5)	2.2 (0.7)[a]	2.3 (0.3)[a]	2.5 (0.4)[b]
Psychosocial interventions***	1.9 (0.8)	1.7 (1.0)[a]	2.0 (0.5)[b]	2.1 (0.8)[b]
Treatment planning/ monitoring***	1.8 (0.8)	1.6 (1.0)[a]	1.9 (0.5)[b]	2.1 (0.7)[c]
Outreach/resilience**	1.9 (0.9)	1.8 (1.1)[a]	2.0 (0.6)[a]	2.2 (0.7)[b]

NOTES: ** $p < 0.01$, *** $p < 0.001$. Values with differing letter superscripts within rows are statistically different at the $p < 0.05$ level, according to post hoc paired comparisons. Overall: $n = 517$–527; Army: $n = 186$–188; Navy: $n = 100$–102; Air Force: $n = 237$–238.

observed (not reported). Furthermore, we expected that BHTs who deployed in the previous 12 months may have perceived themselves as more proficient in some types of tasks, given anecdotal reports of expanded autonomy in deployed settings. However, there were no significant differences in self-reported proficiency levels between BHTs who deployed in the previous 12 months and those who did not.

Variation in BHT Self-Reported Proficiency and Practice Attributes

We also examined whether there was an association between BHTs' reported level of proficiency in performing various types of tasks and the amount of time they had been in practice, as well as the amount of time they spent on patient care activities in a typical week (Table 5.2). We expected those with more experience as BHTs and those who spent more time on patient care to be more proficient in performing clinical tasks. There was a moderate positive correlation between the amount of time BHTs had been practicing and BHTs' reported proficiency in performing tasks, particularly for psychosocial interventions ($r = 0.48$), treatment planning/monitoring tasks ($r = 0.47$), and outreach and resilience activities ($r = 0.49$). In contrast, there was no significant association between BHTs' level of proficiency and the amount of time BHTs spent on patient care activities across all task subscores.

TABLE 5.2

Association Between BHT-Reported Proficiency in Performing Tasks and Practice Attributes

Subscore	BHT Time in Practice (correlation)	BHT Time Spent on Patient Care Activities (correlation)
Screening/assessment	0.31***	−0.05
Psychosocial interventions	0.48***	0.02
Treatment planning/ monitoring	0.47***	−0.08
Outreach/resilience	0.49***	−0.12

NOTES: *** $p < 0.001$. Screening/assessment: $n = 528$; psychosocial interventions: $n = 528$; treatment planning/monitoring: $n = 527$; outreach/resilience: $n = 523$.

Summary

Our findings demonstrate that BHTs perceive themselves to be most proficient at screening and assessment tasks such as conducting risk assessments, triaging walk-in patients, and conducting intake interviews. On the other hand, BHTs reported being least proficient at assessing medication adherence and side effects and administering and scoring cognitive and neuropsychological tests. Although we observed significantly higher self-reported proficiency at tasks by Air Force BHTs, there were no significant differences in BHT responses based on current assignment or deployment history. Finally, we found a moderate positive correlation between BHTs' perceived proficiency and the amount of time they had been in practice, yet there were no significant differences based on the amount of time BHTs spent on patient care.

MHP-Reported Proficiency in Performing Clinical Tasks

To parallel the series of questions regarding BHT-reported proficiency for performing tasks, MHPs were asked to report how proficient they perceived BHTs to be in performing each of the clinical tasks. Response options ranged from "They cannot perform this task" to "They can perform this task with no assistance and they can train someone to perform this task." Figure 5.2 summarizes the percentage of MHPs who reported that BHTs could perform each task with no assistance or perform the task with no assistance and train others on the task.

The largest proportion of MHPs perceived BHTs to be proficient at using the Behavioral Health Data Portal (73 percent) and administering and scoring symptom measures (68 percent). In addition, about half of MHPs indicated that they perceived BHTs as proficient at triaging walk-in patients, conducting behavioral health outreach, and conducting intake interviews.

We also examined the proportion of MHPs who indicated that BHTs cannot perform a given task (Table E.4 in Appendix E). This included administering and scoring neuropsychological or cognitive tests (68 percent), delivering EBP for substance use disorders (53 percent), assessing medication adherence and side effects (53 percent), and delivering EBP for mental health concerns (52 percent).

FIGURE 5.2

Percentage of MHPs Who Reported That BHTs Could Perform a Task with No Assistance and Could Train Someone Else on That Task

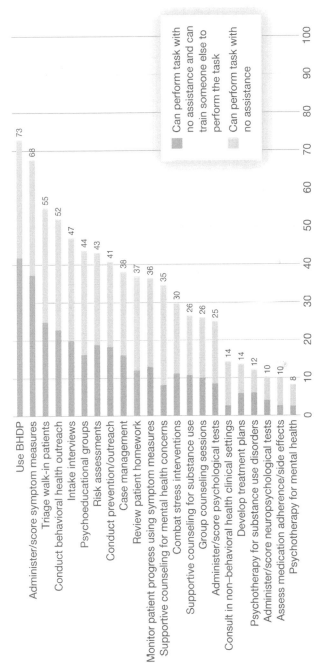

Percentage of MHPs reporting that BHTs could perform tasks with no assistance or perform tasks with no assistance and train someone else

NOTE: n = 593–663.

Variation in MHP-Reported Proficiency Overall and by Service Branch

In this section, we examine whether MHPs' perceptions of BHT proficiency varied by service branch. For these analyses, we also computed four subscores reflecting MHP reports of BHT proficiency for screening/assessment, psychosocial interventions, treatment planning/monitoring, and outreach/resilience tasks. (See Table B.2 in Appendix B for item assignment to subscores.) Internal consistency reliability (Cronbach's alpha) for the subscores ranged from 0.79 (screening/assessment) to 0.84 (psychosocial intervention, outreach/resilience). Correlations between subscores ranged from 0.52 (between screening/assessment and outreach/resilience) and 0.76 (between psychosocial intervention and treatment planning/monitoring).

Table 5.3 describes MHPs perception of BHTs' proficiency with each of the four task subscores, as well as the variation in perceptions across service branches. MHPs reported the highest perceived BHT proficiency for screening/assessment-related tasks. There was some variability by service branch, as MHPs in the Air Force gave BHTs significantly higher proficiency ratings than Army and Navy MHPs.

TABLE 5.3

MHP-Reported BHT Proficiency in Performing Tasks, Overall and by Service Branch

Subscore	Mean (SD)			
	Overall	Army	Navy	Air Force
Screening/assessment***	1.5 (0.6)	1.4 (0.7)[a]	1.5 (0.5)[a]	1.7 (0.6)[b]
Psychosocial interventions***	1.1 (0.7)	0.9 (0.7)[a]	1.0 (0.5)[a]	1.4 (0.6)[b]
Treatment planning/ monitoring***	1.1 (0.7)	0.9 (0.7)[a]	1.1 (0.5)[b]	1.4 (0.7)[c]
Outreach/resilience***	1.2 (0.8)	1.0 (0.8)[a]	1.2 (0.6)[b]	1.8 (0.7)[c]

NOTES: *** $p < 0.001$. Values with differing letter superscripts within rows are statistically different at the $p < 0.05$ level, according to post hoc paired comparisons. Screening/assessment: $n = 670$; psychosocial interventions: $n = 655$; treatment planning/monitoring: $n = 651$; outreach/resilience: $n = 643$.

Variation in MHP-Reported Proficiency by Provider Type, Military Status, Supervisor Status, and Deployment History

In addition to variation in MHP-reported proficiency by service branch, we examined whether MHPs differed in their responses according to their area of clinical practice, military status, supervisor status, and deployment history. Perceptions of BHT proficiency did not vary significantly by provider type, but active-duty MHPs reported higher levels of BHT proficiency compared to civilian providers across subscores ($p < 0.01$ to < 0.001). MHPs who supervised BHTs also reported higher levels of proficiency compared to those who do not ($p < 0.05$). It may be that MHPs who had worked more closely with BHTs had a better sense of their skill level and that active-duty MHPs were more familiar with the model of working alongside enlisted service members or had a more concrete sense of their skill-level or training. There were no differences in levels of proficiency reported by MHPs who had deployed with a BHT in the previous 12 months compared with those who had not.

Concordance Between MHP-Reported Proficiency and Practice Attributes

We examined whether the amount of time that MHPs have been in practice was associated with their perceptions of BHT proficiency. On the one hand, those in practice longer might perceive BHTs as more proficient because they might have more experience working alongside junior clinicians and/or BHTs, and therefore have more realistic expectations regarding their skill set. However, they might also be further from training themselves and therefore have less awareness of the amount of OJT needed to further develop BHTs' skills. We anticipated that time in practice in the MHS may have a stronger association with perceptions of proficiency than overall time in practice, as it is unlikely MHPs opportunities to work with individuals in analogous positions to BHTs in civilian settings.

Across all subscores, there was a small negative association between MHP time in practice and MHP-reported level of proficiency for BHT tasks (Table 5.4). There were small negative correlations between MHP time in practice and perceptions of BHT proficiency for screening/assessment, psychosocial interventions, and treatment planning/monitoring. By contrast, contrary to expectations, correlations between MHP time in practice in the

TABLE 5.4

Association Between MHP-Reported BHT Proficiency in Performing Tasks and Practice Attributes

Subscore	MHP Time in Practice (correlation)	MHP Time in Practice in the MHS (correlation)
Screening/assessment	−0.13***	−0.07
Psychosocial interventions	−0.17***	−0.08
Treatment planning/ monitoring	−0.10**	−0.06
Outreach/resilience	−0.08	0.04

NOTES: ** $p < 0.01$, *** $p < 0.001$. Screening/assessment: $n = 670$; psychosocial interventions: $n = 655$; treatment planning/monitoring: $n = 651$; outreach/resilience: $n = 643$.

MHS and MHP-reported proficiency of BHT tasks were nonsignificant. It may be that MHPs who have been in practice longer have higher expectations for what BHTs should be capable of, though it is important to note that these correlations were small.

Summary

MHPs perceived BHTs to be particularly proficient at using the Behavioral Health Data Portal and administering and scoring symptom measures and least proficient at administering and scoring neuropsychological or cognitive tests. We also observed significantly higher perceived levels of proficiency of tasks by MHPs for Air Force BHTs compared to Army and Navy BHTs. Regarding MHP characteristics, there were significant differences in perceptions of BHT proficiency by military status and supervisor status, and no significant differences by provider type or deployment history. Furthermore, there was a small negative association between MHP-reported BHT proficiency and time in practice as an MHP. Yet, there were no significant correlations with the amount of time MHPs specifically spent practicing in the MHS.

Concordance Between BHT-Reported Proficiency and MHP-Reported Proficiency

We conducted a series of analyses to better understand the concordance between BHT-reported proficiency and MHP-reported proficiency on each task. There was a large significant association between mean BHT item scores and MHP item scores ($r = 0.88$) across the 22 items ($p < 0.001$). We further analyzed the correlation between BHT and MHP item scores by service branch. Correlations ranged from 0.78 for the Air Force to 0.88 for the Army ($p < 0.001$). This suggests that BHTs and MHPs are generally in agreement about the types of tasks that BHTs are able to perform. However, a series of t-tests indicated that across all tasks, there was a significant discrepancy between BHT-reported proficiency and MHP-reported proficiency. Specifically, the mean BHT-reported proficiency rating was significantly higher than the mean MHP-reported proficiency rating across all tasks (results not shown). Furthermore, an examination of discrepancies by service branch did not reveal any clear patterns (analysis not shown).

We then examined the discrepancy between BHT and MHP ratings of BHTs' ability to perform a task with no assistance and/or train someone else on that task. The five items with the highest discrepancy are summarized in Figure 5.3. The magnitude of the discrepancy was quite high across these five tasks, ranging from 41.9 percent (for delivering EBP for mental health concerns) to 53.6 percent (for risk assessments). Of note, two of these tasks (performing risk assessments and intake interviews) are among the top five most frequently performed BHT tasks.

Relationship Between Frequency and Perceived Proficiency

Next, we examined the association between BHTs' self-reported proficiency in performing various tasks in relation to the frequency at which they perform them, as well as the association between MHP-reported frequency and perceptions of proficiency (Table 5.5). We expected there to be a fairly strong relationship between BHTs' reported frequency of tasks and their self-reported proficiency because it is likely that as BHTs perform certain tasks more often, they become more confident and proficient in performing

FIGURE 5.3
Top Five Discrepancies Between BHT and MHP Perceptions of BHT Proficiency

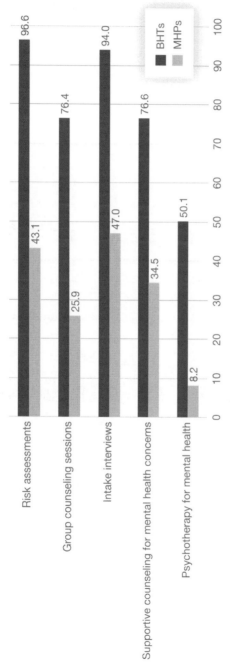

Percentage reporting that BHTs could perform tasks with no assistance or perform tasks with no assistance and train someone else

NOTES: BHTs: *n* = 522–527; MHPs: *n* = 626–659.

TABLE 5.5
Association Between Frequency of Tasks and Proficiency

Task Domain	Correlation Between BHT-Reported Frequency and Self-Reported Proficiency	Correlation Between MHP-Reported Frequency and Perceived Proficiency
Screening/assessment	0.43***	0.67***
Psychosocial interventions	0.60***	0.78***
Treatment planning/ monitoring	0.57***	0.77***
Outreach/resilience	0.57***	0.80***

NOTES: *** $p < 0.001$. Values with differing letter superscripts within rows are statistically different at the $p < 0.05$ level, according to post hoc paired comparisons. Screening/assessment: BHTs: $n = 528$; MHPs: $n = 670$. Psychosocial interventions: BHTs: $n = 528$; MHPs: $n = 655$. Treatment planning/ monitoring: BHTs: $n = 527$; MHPs: $n = 651$. Outreach/resilience: BHTs: $n = 523$; MHPs: $n = 643$.

that task. For similar reasons, we anticipated there might be a strong association between the frequency with which MHPs observe BHTs completing tasks and their perceptions of BHT proficiency.

There were moderate correlations between BHTs' self-reported level of proficiency and the frequency with which they perform tasks across subscores. We computed similar calculations for the relationship between MHPs' reported frequency of tasks and their perceptions of BHTs' level of proficiency with those tasks. There were moderate to high correlations between MHP perceptions of BHT proficiency and the frequency with which the BHTs they work with perform tasks.

Changes in Responsibilities During Deployment

As mentioned, about 12 percent of BHTs reported serving in a deployed setting in the previous 12 months. Of those, roughly 55 percent had deployed with a medical unit, and 45 percent had deployed with an operational unit (Table 5.6). Although there were some differences across branches of service (e.g., the Navy had the highest proportion of BHTs deployed with medical units, whereas the Air Force had the highest proportion deployed with operational units), these differences were not statistically significant.

TABLE 5.6

Type of Deployment, Overall and by Service Branch

Type of Unit	Overall (%) $n = 70$	Army (%) $n = 24$	Navy (%) $n = 34$	Air Force (%) $n = 12$
Medical unit	55.1	56.2	63.2	NR
Operational unit	44.9	43.8	36.8	63.4

NOTE: NR = not reportable.

We examined whether the frequency with which BHTs perform certain tasks changed when they were in deployed settings. BHTs indicated whether they performed each category of tasks more often, less often, or about the same amount of time while deployed as compared to times they were assigned to an MTF in garrison. About 11 percent of those who had deployed indicated that they had not worked in an MTF in garrison before, and therefore were not included in these analyses.

About 50 percent of BHTs reported conducting screening and assessment tasks, psychosocial interventions, and outreach and resilience tasks more often while deployed. In contrast, about half of BHTs indicated that they perform treatment planning/monitoring tasks less often while deployed. Fewer than 20 percent of BHTs noted that the frequency remained the same across all subscores. Though we are unable to quantify how much more—or less—often they conducted tasks in each of these categories, this pattern of responses suggests that responsibilities may shift when BHTs are deployed (Figure 5.4).

Out-of-Scope Responsibilities

Finally, BHTs reported whether they had been asked to perform a task that exceeded their training or that they perceived to be outside their scope of practice. In total, about 44 percent reported that they had been asked to practice outside their scope, primarily when in garrison settings (Table 5.7). On a parallel question, about 20 percent of MHPs reported that they had observed BHTs performing a task that they perceived outside their scope of practice, also largely in garrison settings. In part, this may reflect the relatively greater amount of time that BHTs spend in garrison settings.

FIGURE 5.4

BHT-Reported Frequency of Tasks While Deployed

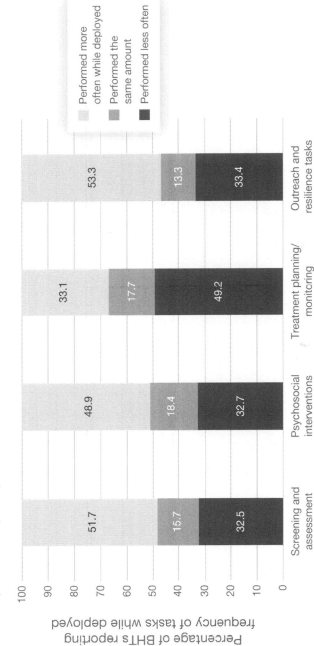

NOTE: *n* = 68–69.

TABLE 5.7

Settings in Which BHTs Practiced Outside of Scope

Setting	BHTs (%) $n = 526$	MHPs (%) $n = 661$
In deployed settings	3.7	4.4
In garrison settings	30.5	11.2
In deployed settings and in garrison	9.6	4.6

Respondents who indicated that they had been asked to perform tasks outside of scope or had observed BHTs performing tasks outside their scope were asked to describe these tasks in more detail. Responses were coded by two members of the research team. The final set of codes and a brief description of each appears in Table 5.8. Of note, these codes were based on the respondent comments and not on an objective evaluation as to whether a task is out of scope for a BHT (i.e., we did not attempt to determine whether a task is actually outside of scope for a BHT versus whether a respondent perceived a task as out of scope). In part, this is because the BHT role encompasses a range of responsibilities which can vary broadly by setting and supervisor, and open-ended responses often did not have the level of detail needed to formally compare the descriptions to existing policy documents guiding BHT practice.

Regarding the type of task, the most common out-of-scope tasks related to treatment and psychotherapy ($n = 117$). A similar number of BHTs and MHPs provided comments that were coded in this category. This included situations in which BHTs were asked to perform mental health or substance use treatment, lead psychoeducational and therapy groups, and carry their own caseload (e.g., in deployed settings). The next most common category of tasks was nonclinical tasks ($n = 54$), which included administrative clinic responsibilities, patient transport, and research. Substantially more BHTs reported completing these types of nonclinical tasks. It may be that BHTs are more likely to perceive these tasks as outside their scope than MHPs, but may also reflect a lack of knowledge on the part of MHPs as to how much nonclinical work BHTs perform. The third most common code was medication-related activities ($n = 43$). These types of tasks were described by both BHTs and MHPs. BHTs especially raised concerns about

TABLE 5.8

Qualitative Coding of Out-of-Scope Activities

Code	Code Description	Number Endorsing Code
Type of task		
Triage and intake	Tasks related to conducting initial evaluations of patients to make decisions about level of care, conducting intake interviews	18
Screening, assessment, and testing	Administration of validated behavioral health screening measures, administration and interpretation of psychological and neuropsychological testing	34
Risk assessment	Completion of risk and safety assessments, including validated suicide risk screening measures	24
Diagnosis	Diagnosing patients	19
Treatment and psychotherapy	Tasks related to mental health and substance use treatment, including supportive counseling, evidence-based practices, group and individual treatment, and psychoeducation	117
Treatment planning	Establishing treatment plans and making treatment recommendations	12
Case management	Case management, care coordination, and identifying additional treatment options	10
Medication-related activities	Administering, monitoring, assessing adherence, and recommending medications	43
Outreach and resilience	Consulting with command, conducting walkabouts, having informal conversations with unit members, providing resilience-oriented briefings	21
Traumatic event management	Implementing Traumatic Event Management, briefing units after traumatic events (e.g., unit member suicide)	7
Other behavioral health tasks	Included such tasks as providing briefings and engaging in specialty training exercises	26
Non–behavioral health clinical tasks	Included changing bandages, treating wounds, and performing medic duties	31

Table 5.8—Continued

Code	Code Description	Number Endorsing Code
Nonclinical tasks	Included research, patient transport, administrative tasks	54
Training and supervision		
Inadequate or lack of training	Situations in which BHTs had not received training or did not have enough training to complete a task, or learned while completing the task	76
Inadequate or lack of supervision	Situations in which BHTs reported having inadequate supervision for a task, supervision was not available, or supervision was not sought	64
Geographic barriers to supervision	Situations in which BHTs were geographically separated from their supervising provider	18
Other		
Working with patients with severe symptoms	Included situations that involved suicidal patients, psychiatric emergencies, violent patients, and individuals experiencing acute mental health symptoms	37
Providing misinformation to patients	Scenarios in which BHTs provided inaccurate treatment plan or diagnostic information, incorrectly administered EBPs	14

the appropriateness of recommending medications and performing medication management (e.g., assessing adherence, assessing effects).

A number of comments related to screening and assessment tasks, which are among the most common BHT responsibilities. BHTs and MHPs provided comments related to triage decisions; intake interviews, screening, assessment, and testing; and risk assessments. Often, the concern raised was that these tasks were performed without adequate supervision, either because supervision was not available or supervision was not sought. A smaller number of respondents provided comments that were coded as treatment planning or case management, or as outreach and resilience. Many of the out-of-scope outreach and resilience tasks were provided by BHTs who described performing command consultation.

In many cases ($n = 37$), part of the reason that a task was described as out of scope was because it involved a severe or high acuity patient. This included suicidal patients, individuals with acute psychiatric symptoms, and violent or homicidal patients. This concern was raised most often by BHTs.

Our question specifically asked about the type of task that was out of scope. However, many of the comments included themes related to training and supervision. There were 76 comments that included references to BHTs having inadequate training to perform a task, most of which were made by BHTs ($n = 60$). This included instances in which BHTs indicated that a task was beyond their training, as well as tasks on which they had not yet been trained but would have felt comfortable performing if training had been provided first. There were also a number of comments referencing a lack of supervision ($n = 61$). This code was applied almost evenly to comments by BHTs and MHPs. When this code was applied to comments from BHTs, it often pertained to a situation in which a provider was not available or the BHT was expected to operate autonomously. Because BHTs are not credentialed, they must practice under the supervision of a licensed MHP; however, there was generally not enough information in the responses to determine whether supervision was completely unavailable or just perceived as less available in the moment. When the code was applied to comments from MHPs, it generally indicated scenarios in which a BHT failed to seek supervision or consultation from an MHP before making an important triage or treatment decision, whether or not the situation came to the attention of a supervisor at a later time.

Though not common, a small number of comments described situations in which BHTs had provided inaccurate information to patients or had inappropriately applied clinical techniques. MHPs described instances in which information given by BHTs to patients conflicted with the guidance that the MHP would have provided.

Summary

This chapter explored BHTs' and MHPs' perceptions of BHTs' competence across a range of tasks. Regarding their confidence to complete clinical tasks, BHTs indicated that they are most proficient performing screening and assessment activities—the tasks that they performed most often in clinical settings. They reported less proficiency with tasks that they performed infrequently, such as assessing medications or administering neuropsychological tests. The relationship between frequency and self-reported proficiency likely indicates that BHTs feel less confident performing tasks that they do infrequently. However, it is also possible that their lack of perceived proficiency with certain tasks—possibly resulting from limited formal training in those tasks—shaped their engagement, at least in settings in which they had more influence over their clinical responsibilities. Air Force BHTs tended to perceive themselves as most proficient across categories of tasks, which again, could reflect their well-defined career standards.

BHT- and MHP-rated proficiency were correlated across tasks, suggesting that BHTs and MHPs generally agreed about the types of tasks that BHTs were most equipped to perform. However, it is notable that MHPs did not perceive BHTs to be as proficient as BHTs seemed to feel, as evidenced by the large discrepancies between BHT- and MHP-rated proficiency. Moreover, the magnitude of the discrepancy was quite high even for some of those tasks that BHTs do most often, like conducting risk assessments. MHPs who perceive the BHTs they work with to be more competent may be more likely to integrate them in a meaningful way into clinical activities. Addressing this discrepancy may require a combination of efforts. It could include identifying ways to increase BHT skills for certain tasks but might also involve the need to address a mismatch between MHP expectations and BHT competencies. Our findings in Chapter Seven, regarding barriers to integrating BHTs into clinical tasks and potential solutions, provide more insight into these potential solutions. That said, certain groups of MHPs appeared to perceive BHTs as more proficient, including Air Force MHPs, active-duty MHPs, and those who supervised BHTs.

When BHTs deployed, about half reported that they performed screening and assessment, psychosocial interventions, and outreach and resilience more often than in an MTF in garrison. However, treatment planning and monitoring tasks were performed less often. Across all tasks, relatively few BHTs reported that the time they spent on tasks was about the same as an MTF in garrison. This supports previous findings suggesting that the BHT role changes during deployment. One concern that has been raised about limiting BHT time in patient care activities while in garrison is that it prevents BHTs from developing the skills they use while deployed. These findings indicate that skill development in the screening and assessment, psychosocial interventions, and outreach and resilience domains could help ensure that BHTs are prepared to deploy.

About 44 percent of BHTs reported that they had been asked to perform a task outside their scope of practice, and about 20 percent of MHPs reported they had observed BHTs performing a task outside their scope of practice. Most of these instances were observed in garrison settings. The most common out-of-scope tasks related to treatment and psychotherapy, followed by nonclinical tasks and medication-related activities. Out-of-scope tasks related to other categories of BHT tasks—including screening/assessment, treatment planning and monitoring, and outreach/resilience—were less common. It may be that there is more consensus about the role that BHTs should play in these types of tasks, compared to tasks relating to psychosocial interventions (e.g., supportive counseling, EBP). In these open-ended responses, BHTs and MHPs commonly referenced concerns about BHTs not having adequate training or supervision to perform certain tasks, either because supervision was unavailable or because BHTs did not seek supervision. In the next chapter, we examine BHT and MHP perceptions of supervision and training in more depth.

CHAPTER SIX

Training and Supervision

In this chapter, we discuss BHT and MHP perceptions of the training and supervision received by BHTs. This includes the perceived adequacy of the time BHTs spend on training in various settings, from their technical training at METC to OJT and continuing education. We also describe perceptions of supervision that BHTs receive.

Perceived Adequacy of BHT Training

BHT Perceptions

BHTs reported their perceptions of the various types of training that they receive, including training received as part of basic BHT training at METC that prepares them to enter the career field, as well as the ongoing training they receive after entering the behavioral health workforce. BHTs indicated whether they spent "too much," "too little," or "about the right amount of time" on each type of training. In this section, we examine BHTs' reported perceptions of adequacy of BHT training, as well as the variation in perceptions by service branch, their time in practice and the amount of time spent in patient care–related activities.

Figure 6.1 illustrates the proportion of BHTs who felt that they do not spend enough time in various training settings. Relatively few BHTs reported that there was insufficient time spent in classroom instruction at METC (14 percent). By contrast, more than half of BHTs indicated that they did not spend enough time in their clinical practicum experience at METC and on continuing education (55 percent and 55 percent, respectively). This suggests that BHTs are interested in undergoing more applied experiences prior to entering the field, which could potentially boost their level of con-

FIGURE 6.1

Percentage of BHTs Who Reported Insufficient BHT Time in Training, Overall and by Service Branch

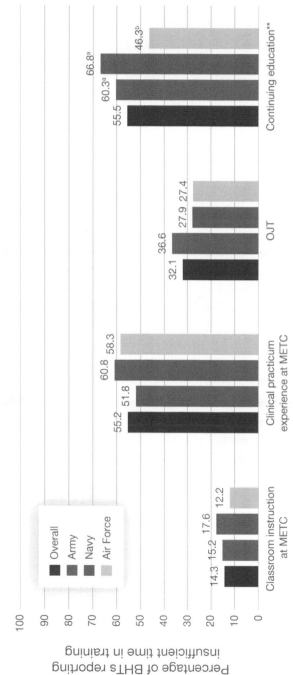

NOTES: ** $p < 0.01$. Values with differing letter superscripts within column clusters are statistically different at the $p < 0.05$ level, according to post hoc paired comparisons. $n = 518–526$.

fidence in performing various tasks. BHTs might also find continuing education useful because they have had a chance to use their skills in clinical settings and identify where there might be gaps in their knowledge or skills.

Relatively few BHTs indicated that they spent "too much time" in each of the training settings. About 17 percent of BHTs reported that they spent "too much time" on classroom instruction at METC (17.4 percent), but fewer than 3 percent of BHTs endorsed spending "too much time" on the other types of trainings.

We also examined service branch differences in BHT perceptions of time spent in training. The only significant differences observed were for continuing education, where fewer Air Force BHTs indicated that they felt as though the amount of time was inadequate (results not shown). This could be because of the Air Force's well-standardized continuing education curriculum for BHTs, which requires BHTs to complete home study courses to be promoted, as well as continuing education for recertification as CADCs every three years (U.S. Air Force, 2015). By comparison, continuing education requirements are somewhat less specific in the other branches (e.g., the Army requires 12 hours of continuing education each year, but it can include a class, self-study, or in-service training, and the topics are not pre-specified) (Headquarters, U.S. Department of the Army, 2017).

In addition to understanding differences by service branch, we analyzed whether BHTs' perceptions of their time in training varied by the amount of time they had practiced as a BHT. BHTs who had completed training within the last two years were less likely to perceive classroom instruction at METC to be inadequate compared to BHTs who had been practicing for more than two years (Table 6.1). We observed a similar trend for BHTs' clinical practicum experience at METC, though it was not statistically significant. This may reflect the fact that as BHTs spend more time in clinical practice, they may have a better understanding of what might not have been covered thoroughly enough at METC. It could also reflect the evolution of training approaches over time.

Finally, we examined differences in how BHTs responded according to the amount of time they spend performing patient care-related activities (Figure 6.2). BHTs who spend little to none of their time in patient care-related activities (0–10 percent) were more likely to endorse "too little time" spent on continuing education (64 percent) and OJT (41 percent). These rat-

TABLE 6.1

Percentage of BHTs Reporting Insufficient BHT Time in Training, by Years in Practice

Type of Training	0–2 Years (%)	2–7 Years (%)	7+ Years (%)
Classroom instruction at METC***	8.3[a]	13.7[b]	19.3[b]
Clinical practicum experience at METC	46.6	54.7	62.1
OJT	31.6	30.8	34.2
Continuing education	47.6	59.9	54.8

NOTES: *** $p < 0.001$. Values with differing letter superscripts within rows are statistically different at the $p < 0.05$ level, according to post hoc paired comparisons. $n = 518–526$.

ings of insufficient OJT might reflect the limited time these BHTs spend on patient care–related activities. However, these responses might also indicate a desire for more structured training experiences to supplement the limited time these BHTs spend on clinical activities.

MHP Perceptions

In addition to gauging BHTs' perceptions of the adequacy of time spent in training, we sought to understand the perceptions of the MHPs who work with BHTs. In this section, we also analyze how MHPs' perceptions varied by service branch, military status, and supervisor status. Compared with BHTs, a greater proportion of MHPs indicated that too little time was spent across training types. This could signify that MHPs perceived BHTs as not entirely prepared for their role by the level of training they received, but it might also reflect limited knowledge of BHTs' training experiences. More than two-thirds of MHPs reported that BHTs were not allotted enough time for their clinical practicum at METC (70 percent) and their continuing education (69 percent), as shown in Figure 6.3. In addition, more than 50 percent of MHPs indicated that the amount of time BHTs spent on OJT was insufficient. This could indicate MHPs' understanding that classroom instruction at METC is supposed to provide foundational skills but that BHTs require additional applied experiences once they enter the workforce.

FIGURE 6.2

Percentage of BHTs Who Reported Insufficient BHT Time in Training, by Time Spent on Patient Care Activities

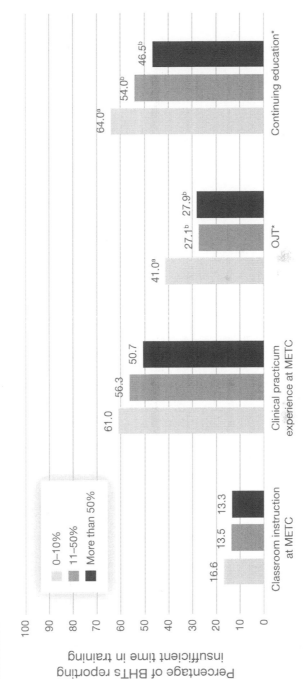

NOTES: * $p < 0.05$. Values with differing letter superscripts within column clusters are statistically different at the $p < 0.05$ level as determined by post hoc paired comparisons. $n = 518–526$.

FIGURE 6.3
Percentage of MHPs Who Reported Insufficient BHT Time in Training, Overall and by Service Branch

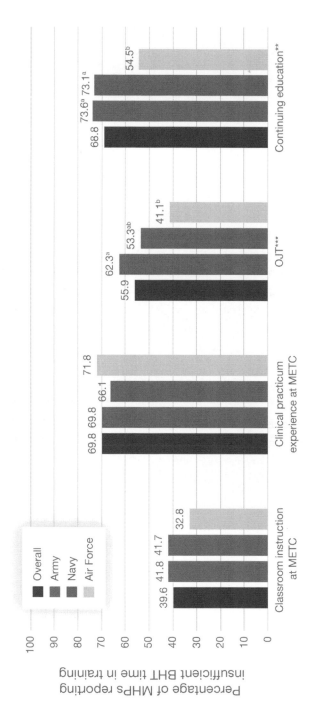

NOTES: ** $p < 0.01$, *** $p < 0.001$. Values with differing letter superscripts within column clusters are statistically different at the $p < 0.05$ level, according to post hoc paired comparisons. $n = 239$–561.

Across all training types, less than 6 percent of MHPs reported that there was too much time spent on training.

Figure 6.3 shows that there was some variation in MHPs' perceptions of time in training across service branches. Similar to the pattern observed in BHTs, a smaller proportion of MHPs in the Air Force reported that continuing education was inadequate. Again, this could be a result of the Air Force's specific standards regarding the continuing education required for career progression. In addition, significantly fewer Air Force MHPs perceived time on OJT as inadequate compared with Army MHPs.

We also evaluated variation in perceptions among MHPs by military status. Civilian MHPs were more likely to report that BHTs did not spend enough time in classroom instruction at METC (43.1 percent) compared to active-duty MHPs (36.6 percent, $p < 0.05$). On the other hand, more than three-quarters of active-duty MHPs (76.0 percent) indicated that BHTs spent an insufficient amount of time on continuing education activities, while nearly two-thirds of civilian MHPs did so (60.7 percent, $p < 0.01$).

In addition, significant differences were observed between MHPs who supervised BHTs and those who did not ($p < 0.05$). More non-supervisors reported that BHTs spend the right amount of time on OJT (45.6 percent) compared with supervisors (38.7 percent). Similarly, supervisors were more likely to report that BHTs spent too little time on continuing education (73.8 percent) than non-supervisors (63.9 percent, $p < 0.05$). MHPs who are supervisors may have a greater tendency to report that BHTs spend too little time in certain types of training because they are overseeing BHTs and might be more aware of their skills in performing various clinical tasks.

Perceived Adequacy of BHT Supervision

To provide further clarity on perceptions of the supervision that BHTs receive, we asked both BHTs and MHPs whether BHTs received adequate supervision to perform clinical duties. Response options were "yes," "no," and "unsure." In this section, we also examine variations in the perceived adequacy of BHT supervision by BHT and MHP service branch and discuss significant differences among BHTs by their time in practice, the type of provider that they supported, and the amount of time they spent on patient care. Finally, we analyzed variations in MHPs' perceptions based on their military and supervisor status.

Figure 6.4 demonstrates the stark differences that we observed between BHTs and MHPs with respect to perceptions of supervision. About 15 percent of BHTs reported feeling as though they did not receive adequate supervision, whereas 40 percent of MHPs reported that they did not think BHTs received adequate supervision. MHPs' tendency to indicate that BHTs did not receive adequate supervision might reflect their perceptions that BHTs were not entirely proficient at performing certain tasks and might need greater oversight. On the other hand, BHTs might have felt that they generally had enough supervision, which aligns with BHTs' high level of confidence in performing certain tasks, as described in Chapter Five.

In addition to examining the proportion who responded that BHTs did not receive enough supervision, we explored the proportion of BHTs who reported that they are unsure if they receive adequate supervision, and the proportion of MHPs who reported that they are unsure if BHTs receive adequate supervision (Table E.5 in Appendix E). About 16.3 percent of MHPs

FIGURE 6.4

Percentage of BHTs and MHPs Who Indicated That BHTs Did Not Receive Adequate Supervision, Overall and by Service Branch

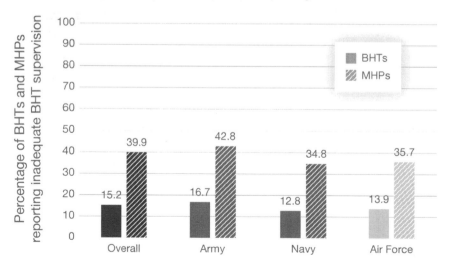

NOTES: BHTs: n = 526; MHPs: n = 657.

reported that they were unsure whether BHTs receive adequate supervision. This may reflect the lack of standardized policies related to supervision of BHTs. However, it might also reflect uncertainty on the part of providers regarding expected BHT skills. For example, they may be unsure if BHTs should be practicing at a higher level or if BHTs are practicing at their expected skill level, which, in turn, might influence their perceptions regarding supervision needs. On the other hand, only 7 percent of BHTs reported being unsure whether they received enough supervision.

For the remaining analyses in this section, we include only "yes" or "no" response options to explore the dichotomy between those who reported feeling as though they do or do not receive adequate supervision. Figure 6.4 also illustrates perceptions of supervision by service branch. There were no significant differences in perceptions across service branches for BHTs or MHPs.

We conducted supplemental analyses to assess whether there were significant differences in the percentage of BHTs and MHPs reporting that supervision was adequate versus inadequate. Among BHTs, there were no significant differences with respect to time in practice as a BHT or type of provider supported. There was a significant difference with respect to time spent in patient care ($p < 0.01$), with those spending more time on patient care activities more likely to perceive supervision as adequate. This finding aligns with our previous finding that BHTs who spend little time in patient care–related activities tend to feel as though there is not sufficient time spent in OJT and continuing education.

Among MHPs, there was no significant difference in perceptions of supervision for active-duty versus civilian MHPs. A higher proportion of supervisors felt that BHTs receive adequate supervision (53.6 percent) compared to non-supervisors (36.8 percent, $p < 0.01$). It is likely that MHPs who supervise BHTs feel as though they are providing valuable and sufficient supervision to the best of their ability, though this still leaves a notable percentage who indicated that supervision was not adequate.

Summary

This chapter focused on perceptions of the adequacy of training received by BHTs. BHT training begins at METC, beginning with several weeks of classroom instruction followed by a clinical practicum experience. Given the amount of material covered during the classroom component of METC training, it is difficult to cover any topic in much detail (Holliday et al., 2019). However, about 84 percent of BHTs reported that they spent the right amount of time or too much time in the classroom. About 60 percent of MHPs also reported that classroom time was adequate or more than adequate, though it is unclear how familiar MHPs are with the training that BHTs receive while at METC. That said, it may be that BHTs and MHPs understand that the classroom experience is meant to provide an initial introduction to the skills BHTs will use in the workforce, and that additional training will be needed to continue developing those skills. An interesting relationship was observed between perceptions of classroom instruction and time that BHTs have been in practice. Those BHTs who had been in practice for more than two years were more likely to report that not enough time was spent on classroom instruction than those who had been in practice less than two years. It may be that once BHTs spend more time in the workforce, they have a better sense of the types of patients they encounter most often or the clinical skills they use most often, and believe more METC classroom time could be spent on these types of topics.

Though most BHTs and MHPs perceived METC classroom instruction to be adequate, about half of BHTs and nearly 70 percent of MHPs reported that not enough time was spent on the practicum experience. Practicum training varies in duration across services but is relatively short, ranging from 2.5 to 5.1 weeks (Clay, 2016). During the practicum experience, BHTs typically practice writing clinical notes, facilitate psychoeducational groups, and conduct a case presentation. These types of practical training experiences provide a valuable opportunity to apply skills learned in the classroom, above and beyond classroom roleplays. Therefore, this finding might reflect a desire for more applied experiences before BHTs complete their technical training.

BHTs continue to participate in training once they enter the workforce, including OJT and more structured continuing education. In general, a higher percentage of MHPs than BHTs reported that not enough time is spent on these training activities. However, about one-third of BHTs reported that they did not spend enough time on OJT, and about half reported insufficient time spent on continuing education. There were some differences by service branch; in particular, a smaller proportion of BHTs and MHPs in the Air Force reported that not enough time was spent on continuing education. This might be indicative of the more-standardized continuing education curriculum for Air Force BHTs. In addition, a greater proportion of MHPs who supervised BHTs (and who likely had greater awareness of BHTs' skill levels) reported that not enough time is spent on continuing education.

Clinical supervision is an important component of ongoing skill development for BHTs. About 15 percent of BHTs and 40 percent of MHPs reported that BHTs do not receive adequate supervision. In part, this could reflect the discrepancy between BHTs' self-reported proficiency in performing clinical tasks and MHPs' perceptions of BHTs' proficiency in performing those same tasks, as described in Chapter Five. That said, BHTs who spend the least amount of time on patient care activities were more likely to indicate that they did not receive adequate supervision. Given that all MHPs responding to the survey had worked with a BHT in the previous month, a surprising proportion of MHPs reported that they were unsure whether BHTs received enough supervision (about 16 percent). This could reflect the lack of standardized requirements for supervision and uncertainty about the level at which BHTs should be performing certain clinical tasks.

CHAPTER SEVEN

Barriers to Effective BHT Practice

In this chapter, we examine potential barriers to effective BHT practice. In our curriculum, policy, and literature review (Holliday et al., 2019), we identified a number of potential barriers to effectively integrating BHTs into clinical settings. These included barriers related to training and supervision needs, the nature of BHT responsibilities, potential variation in BHT skills, and MHP familiarity with BHT capabilities. In surveying BHTs and MHPs, we had the opportunity to further explore their perceptions of the extent to which these barriers inhibited BHTs from applying their skills in clinical settings.

BHT Perspectives on Barriers to BHT Practice

To gain a better understanding of the factors that may affect the types of roles that BHTs fulfill, including the extent to which they are integrated into clinical responsibilities, BHTs were presented with 11 statements reflecting potential barriers and were asked to indicate the extent to which they agreed with each statement. Response options ranged from "strongly disagree" to "strongly agree." Figure 7.1 shows the percentage who agreed or strongly agreed with the barrier statement, sorted by most to least frequently endorsed. The statement that most BHTs agreed with was that "There can be substantial variability in behavioral health technician skills, even within the same rank" (90 percent agreed or strongly agreed). This might reflect the wide range of tasks and responsibilities that BHTs undertake, but it also captures variation in opportunities for ongoing training and supervision. Other common barriers included the belief that MHPs would be more comfortable sharing tasks with BHTs if they had a credential, that MHPs

FIGURE 7.1

Percentage of BHTs Who Agreed or Strongly Agreed with Statements About Barriers to Effective BHT Practice

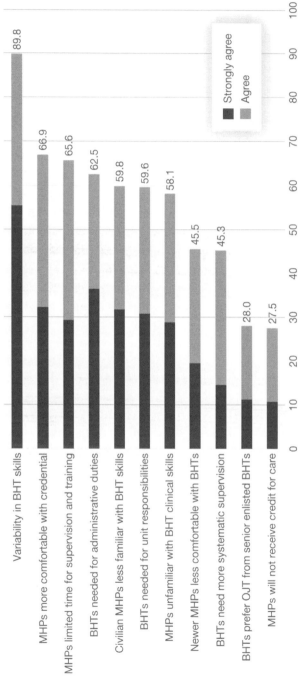

Percentage of BHTs who agreed or strongly agreed

NOTE: *n* = 525–526.

have limited time to supervise BHTs, and that BHTs are often tasked with administrative responsibilities.

We also evaluated the degree to which BHTs disagreed with this set of statements (Appendix Figure E.6). Notably, nearly 50 percent of BHTs strongly disagreed or disagreed that "If licensed mental health providers integrate behavioral health technicians more into clinical care more, they won't get credit for delivering the care."

We also conducted analyses to evaluate whether differences in perceived barriers existed across service branches or time in practice as a BHT. We provide an overview of findings here, and complete tables of results can be found in Appendix E. Across services branches, the top endorsed barrier to effective BHT practice was the variability in BHT skills, even within the same rank (Table E.1 in Appendix E). There were some differences in other top barriers across service branches. For example, the second most common barrier among Army BHTs was that MHPs would feel more comfortable sharing tasks with BHTs if they had a credential, whereas Navy and Air Force BHTs indicated the limited time that MHPs have to invest in supervising and training BHTs, followed by the perception that civilian MHPs are less familiar with BHTs' capabilities. Although there was variation in the order in which barriers were endorsed, there were few significant differences in responses across service branches. However, Air Force BHTs were significantly more likely to indicate a need for more-systematic supervision to effectively provide clinical care ($p < 0.05$). This echoes our previous findings that Air Force BHTs tend to spend less time on patient care–related clinical activities than their counterparts in other service branches.

There were also significant differences in BHTs' perceptions of the barriers they encounter based on the amount of time they spent in practice. Across all barriers, BHTs with more years in practice were more likely to "strongly agree" or "agree" (Table E.2 in Appendix E). This phenomenon might indicate that BHTs encounter more of these barriers as they spend more time in the field. We observed an especially large discrepancy in the proportions indicating that BHTs need more-systematic supervision to effectively provide clinical care, which was endorsed by about 26 percent of BHTs in practice for two years or less, compared with 63 percent of those in practice for more than seven years ($p < 0.05$). As BHTs spend more time in practice, they might better understand the benefits of strong clinical supervision. In addition, 34 percent of the newest BHTs indicated that civilian MHPs were less familiar with BHT training, compared with 80 percent of BHTs in practice for more than seven years ($p < 0.05$).

MHP Perspectives on Barriers to BHT Practice

MHPs also indicated their level of agreement with the same eleven statements assessing barriers to effective BHT practice. Figure 7.2 shows the percentage of MHPs who agreed or strongly agreed with each barrier statement, sorted by most to least frequently endorsed. Similar to BHTs, the largest proportion of MHPs agreed or strongly agreed that there can be substantial variability in BHT skills, even within the same rank (93 percent). In addition, nearly 80 percent of MHPs believed that BHTs needed more-systematic supervision to effectively provide clinical care (78 percent). Interestingly, this was even greater than the percentage of MHPs who reported that BHTs did not receive adequate supervision (40 percent).

We also examined the proportion of MHPs who indicated that they disagreed or strongly disagreed with each statement. More than half (59 percent) of MHPs disagreed or strongly disagreed with the statement, "If licensed mental health providers integrate behavioral health technicians more into clinical care, they won't get credit for delivering the care" (Figure E.7 in Appendix E). This finding suggests that many MHPs work in settings in which they have found ways to receive credit for services provided, although about 42 percent were still concerned about receiving credit for care delivered alongside a BHT.

We also conducted analyses to evaluate differences in perceived barriers across service branches, by provider type, and time in practice in the MHS. We provide an overview of findings here, and complete tables of results can be found in Appendix E.

Regarding service branch (Table E.3 in Appendix E), the most commonly endorsed barrier across all service branches was variability in BHT skills, even within the same rank. In the Army and Air Force, the next most common barrier was that BHTs needed more-systematic supervision. In the Navy, the next most common barrier was MHPs' lack of familiarity with the range of activities that BHTs are trained to perform. There were few signifi-

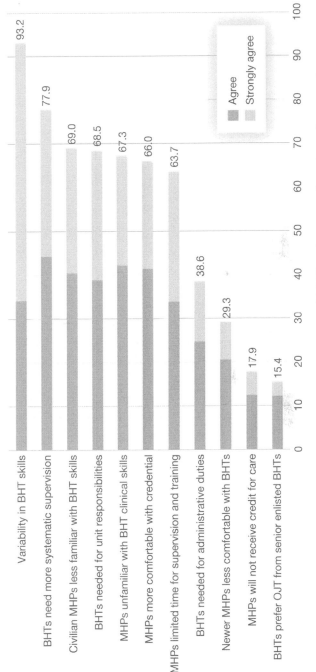

FIGURE 7.2
Percentage of MHPs Who Agreed or Strongly Agreed with Statements About Barriers to Effective BHT Practice

NOTE: n = 652–656.

cant differences in responses across service branches; however, significantly more Air Force MHPs endorsed the idea that MHPs would be more comfortable sharing clinical tasks with BHTs if BHTs had a credential ($p < 0.05$). This might reflect the unique Air Force model, in which all BHTs become certified as CADCs as part of their career progression.

There were few differences with respect to provider type (Table E.4 in Appendix E). However, master's-level clinicians were less likely to indicate that MHPs have limited time to invest in supervision than prescribing providers or doctoral-level psychologists ($p < 0.05$), possibly indicating that providers in these latter groups have additional responsibilities competing for their time. There were also very few differences in perceptions of barriers based on MHPs' time in practice in the MHS (Table E.5).

Finally, there were some differences in MHPs' perceptions of barriers by military status (Table E.6 in Appendix E). A significantly higher proportion of active-duty MHPs reported that civilian MHPs are less familiar than uniformed MHPs with the clinical tasks that BHTs are trained to perform ($p < 0.05$). It may be that active-duty MHPs believe themselves to be more knowledgeable regarding BHTs' responsibilities because of their familiarity with the technical training and expectations for working alongside enlisted personnel. Active-duty MHPs were also more likely to indicate that MHPs have limited time to invest in supervision and training of BHTs ($p < 0.05$), which may reflect that uniformed MHPs also have additional duties (e.g., unit-related responsibilities) to attend to. By contrast, a greater proportion of civilian MHPs endorsed concerns about receiving credit for work performed by BHTs ($p < 0.05$), although, as mentioned earlier, few MHPs endorsed this barrier across groups.

BHT and MHP Agreement on Barriers to Effective Practice

We compared the percentage of BHTs and MHPs who endorsed each of the barriers to identify items with the highest level of agreement and largest discrepancies. Figure 7.3 shows the three barriers with the highest agreement between BHTs and MHPs. About two-thirds of BHTs and MHPs reported that MHPs would be more comfortable sharing clinical tasks with BHTs

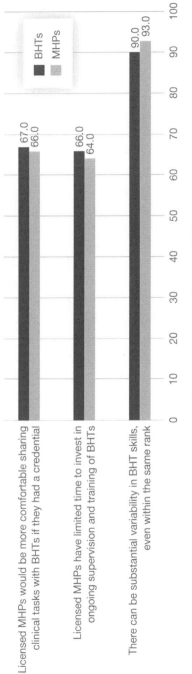

FIGURE 7.3

Barriers with Highest Agreement Between BHTs and MHPs

NOTES: BHTs: *n* = 525–526; MHPs: *n* = 654–656.

if they had a credential and that MHPs have limited time to invest in on-going supervision and training of BHTs. In addition, most BHTs and MHPs agreed that there can be substantial variability in BHT skills, even within the same rank.

Figure 7.4 presents the three barriers with the highest discrepancy between BHT and MHP responses. Most notably, there was a 33 percent difference in the proportion of BHTs and MHPs who believed that BHTs need more systematic supervision to effectively provide clinical care. This parallels our finding (reported in Chapter Six) that a higher percentage of MHPs than BHTs believed that BHTs did not receive enough supervision (40 percent versus 15 percent). However, it is notable that BHTs and MHPs agreed that MHPs have limited time for supervision, but they appeared to disagree on the amount of supervision needed.

We also observed a large discrepancy (24 percent difference) in the proportion of BHTs and MHPs who believe that BHTs are primarily needed for administrative responsibilities, which was endorsed more often by BHTs than MHPs. It may be that MHPs perceive administrative responsibilities to be an expected component of the BHT role or that they do not realize the frequency with which BHTs get asked to complete administrative tasks. However, this disconnect in expectations could affect BHT satisfaction in the longer term.

Finally, a larger proportion of BHTs indicated that more recently trained MHPs are less comfortable working with BHTs. A relatively smaller proportion of both MHPs and BHTs identified this as a barrier. However, this barrier could be addressed through tiered supervision models, which have been implemented in some MTFs. In these models, newer MHPs supervise BHTs. In turn, a more-established MHP provides supervision to the newer MHP, including guidance on how to effectively supervise a BHT, resulting in skill development for the MHP and BHT.

As a final approach to examining the agreement between BHTs and MHPs, we conducted a Spearman rank correlation test to analyze the ranking of barriers by BHTs and MHPs. However, this association was not significant ($r = 0.57$).

FIGURE 7.4

Barriers with Largest Discrepancies Between BHTs and MHPs

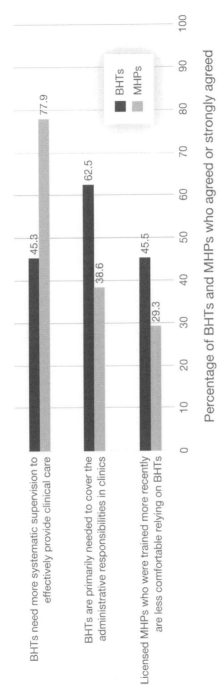

Percentage of BHTs and MHPs who agreed or strongly agreed

NOTES: BHTs: n = 525–526; MHPs: n = 655–656.

Summary

These findings provide insight into BHT and MHP perceptions of the factors that hamper effective BHT practice. Among both BHTs and MHPs, the most commonly endorsed barrier was that there can be variability in BHT skills, even within the same rank. There are a number of factors that can contribute to this variability in BHT skills, including the clinical setting, supervisor preferences, the nature of supervision provided, and amount of time BHTs are able to spend on clinical versus nonclinical tasks. For example, BHTs who have largely worked in substance use treatment settings might have different skills than those who have worked in mental health settings, whereas those who are largely tasked with administrative responsibilities might not have had an opportunity to develop their skills through OJT. This could make it difficult for MHPs to know the best way to integrate BHTs into clinical tasks.

Even if a BHT has not had substantial experience with the tasks needed in a given clinical setting, these skills could be developed with OJT and supervision. Many MHPs reported that BHTs need more-systematic supervision to effectively provide care. Interestingly, this was less commonly endorsed as a barrier by BHTs; however, many BHTs indicated that MHPs do not have enough time to invest in ongoing supervision and training. This suggests that while MHPs see supervision as key to BHT skill development, finding time to provide this supervision could still be an issue. There are few standardized requirements regarding the frequency, intensity, or nature of supervision that MHPs should provide to BHTs. It may be that clearer guidelines for supervision would ensure that MHPs and BHTs have similar expectations for what supervision should look like and accomplish, and such guidance would also help MHPs know how much time to dedicate to supervision.

Both BHTs and MHPs indicated that another barrier can be the lack of time BHTs have available to spend on clinical responsibilities due to other unit responsibilities. BHTs also reported that time spent on administrative responsibilities can be a barrier, though MHPs perceived this as less of a barrier. It may be that MHPs expect that a certain amount of administrative work is a part of the BHT role, but that both BHTs and MHPs agree that time spent outside the clinic setting interferes with effective BHT practice.

To address concerns regarding the balance of clinical and unit responsibilities, Hoyt (2018) suggested that supervising MHPs establish a memorandum of understanding with a BHT's unit commander, which would explicitly outline expectations for time spent in clinic versus time spent on unit-related duties.

BHTs and MHPs indicated that if BHTs had a credential, MHPs might feel more comfortable sharing clinical tasks. This was endorsed more commonly by Air Force MHPs than those in other service branches, likely because all Air Force BHTs become CADCs are part of the standard career progression. Credentialing does have some clear benefits: Those seeking credentials often have to complete specific educational activities and demonstrate competence on specific clinical skills, often under the supervision of a certified or licensed provider.

Our findings suggest some differences in the perceived barriers for active-duty and civilian MHPs. Active-duty MHPs were more likely to report that civilian MHPs are less familiar than uniformed MHPs with the clinical tasks that BHTs are trained to perform. It is unclear whether this simply reflects a perception on the part of active-duty MHPs that they are more familiar with the military training model, or with expectations for working alongside enlisted personnel. However, this is a barrier that could be addressed with better education about BHTs' skills and expectations for their roles. Active-duty MHPs were also more likely to indicate that MHPs have limited time to invest in supervising and training BHTs. It may be that active-duty MHPs have additional duties to balance, such as unit-related responsibilities.

Finally, it is worth examining the barriers that were endorsed by fewest BHTs and MHPs. Only a modest proportion of BHTs and MHPs indicated that BHTs might feel more comfortable receiving OJT from a senior enlisted BHT than from an MHP. This suggests that it is not *who* provides the supervision that matters but, rather, that intentional time is set aside to provide supervision. In addition, relatively fewer BHTs and MHPs indicated that MHPs were concerned that they would not receive credit for care provided alongside a BHT.

CHAPTER EIGHT

Satisfaction

In this chapter, we examine BHT and MHP satisfaction with the BHT role. We begin by examining BHT satisfaction with the nature of their work and the quality of their supervisors. We then explore MHP satisfaction with BHT performance. Finally, we examine the extent to which BHTs believe they are a fit for the BHT role.

BHT Satisfaction

We examined two facets of BHT satisfaction: (1) satisfaction with the type of work they perform and (2) satisfaction with the quality of their supervisor. BHTs were asked to rate their level of satisfaction on a scale ranging from "very satisfied" to "very dissatisfied," with a neutral option of "neither satisfied nor dissatisfied." These items were drawn from DoD's Status of Forces Survey (SOFS) of active-duty members, which uses a large-scale representative sample to evaluate and monitor military personnel programs and policies (Rock, 2020). In this section, we discuss how BHTs rated their satisfaction with their work and the quality of their supervisor, as well as the variation in perceptions of these concepts by BHTs' service branch, time spent practicing as a BHT, and whether they indicated that they did not receive adequate supervision. In addition, we present findings regarding the variation in BHT satisfaction based on the type of provider that a BHT supports and time spent on patient care activities. Finally, we calculate the correlation and analyze the association between BHTs' satisfaction with their work and two variables: (1) frequency with which they perform various types of tasks and (2) their self-reported proficiency in performing those tasks.

Figure 8.1 describes BHTs' overall satisfaction with their work and the quality of their supervisor, as well as their levels of satisfaction by service branch. About 60 percent of BHTs indicated that they were "satisfied" or "very satisfied" with the type of work they perform and the quality of their supervisor. This is similar to the responses of the enlisted population participating in the SOFS, among whom 63 percent indicated they were satisfied with the type of work they perform and 64 percent with the quality of their supervisor (Dorvil, 2017). Although the majority of BHTs are satisfied with their work and supervisor, a quarter of BHTs (25.3 percent) reported that they were not satisfied with the type of work they perform, and about one-fifth of BHTs (19.9 percent) indicated that they were not satisfied with the quality of their supervisor (Figure E.8 in Appendix E).

Regarding service branch differences, Air Force BHTs were less likely than Army BHTs to endorse being satisfied with the type of work they perform ($p < 0.05$). In addition, though not statistically significant, 70 percent of Navy BHTs indicated that they were satisfied with the quality of their

FIGURE 8.1

Percentage of BHTs Who Indicated That They Were Satisfied or Very Satisfied, Overall and by Service Branch

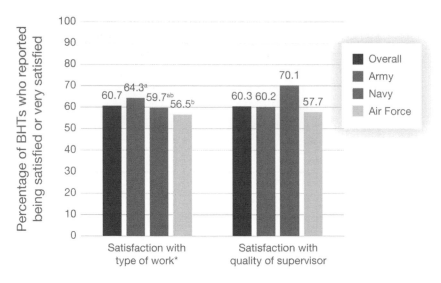

NOTES: * $p < 0.05$. Values with differing letter superscripts within column clusters are statistically different at the $p < 0.05$ level, according to post hoc paired comparisons. $n = 524$.

supervisor, compared to smaller proportions of Army and Air Force BHTs (60 percent and 58 percent, respectively). This difference echoes our findings in Chapter Six, which showed that Navy BHTs were less likely to indicate that their supervision is inadequate, though those findings were not statistically significant.

We also examined whether there were differences in perceptions of satisfaction depending on the amount of time BHTs had spent in practice, but we observed no significant differences (not reported). There were, however, meaningful contrasts between BHTs who reported that they believe they receive adequate supervision and those who do not. Figure 8.2 illustrates that more than two-thirds of BHTs who indicated that they received adequate supervision were also satisfied with both the type of work they performed and the quality of their supervisor. On the other hand, only about a quarter of BHTs who indicated that they do not receive adequate supervision were satisfied with the type of work they were doing (22 percent) and the quality of their supervisor (29 percent). This suggests that the adequacy

FIGURE 8.2

Percentage of BHTs Who Indicated That They Were Satisfied or Very Satisfied, by Perceived Adequacy of Supervision

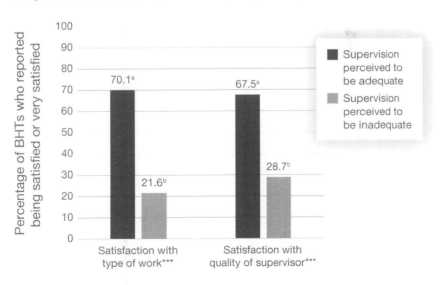

NOTES: *** $p < 0.001$. Values with differing letter superscripts within column clusters are statistically different at the $p < 0.05$ level, according to post hoc paired comparisons. $n = 487$.

of supervision that BHTs receive could play an important role in their job satisfaction.

We examined satisfaction based on the type of providers BHTs supported, but there were no significant differences (results not shown). However, there was significant variation in satisfaction depending on the amount of time BHTs spent on patient care–related activities. As shown in Figure 8.3, BHTs who spent more time performing patient care activities were more likely to be satisfied with their work (for full results, see Figure E.9 in Appendix E). These results suggest that BHTs might perceive their work to be more rewarding and satisfying if they have more opportunities to work directly with patients and fewer administrative responsibilities.

To further assess the extent to which specific BHT responsibilities contribute to BHTs' satisfaction with their work, we examined the association between the frequency with which BHTs perform certain tasks and their reported level of satisfaction. To do so, we used the subscores discussed in

FIGURE 8.3

Percentage of BHTs Satisfied or Very Satisfied with Their Work, by Time Spent on Patient Care

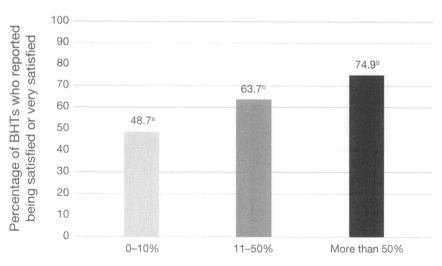

NOTES: *** $p < 0.001$. Values with differing letter superscripts are statistically different at the $p < 0.05$ level, according to post hoc paired comparisons. $n = 489$.

Chapter Four indicating frequency of time spent on screening/assessment, psychosocial intervention, treatment planning/monitoring, and outreach/resilience activities. We observed small but statistically significant correlations with satisfaction with work across these subscores (ranging from $r = 0.10$ for screening/assessment activities to $r = 0.21$ for outreach/resilience) ($p < 0.05$). This is consistent with our previous finding that BHTs who spend more time performing patient care–related activities tend to have greater job satisfaction.

In addition, we calculated the correlation between BHTs' self-reported proficiency in performing various types of tasks and their level of satisfaction with their work. We found small but significant correlations with satisfaction with work for screening/assessment ($r = 0.14$, $p < 0.01$), psychosocial interventions ($r = 0.14$, $p < 0.01$), and outreach/resilience ($r = 0.11$, $p < 0.05$). This suggests that greater self-reported proficiency in performing most types of clinical activities is associated with BHTs' greater satisfaction with their work.

MHP Satisfaction

We likewise surveyed MHPs about their level of satisfaction with the type of work they do in the military and the quality of their supervisor (Table 8.1). About 90 percent of MHPs reported that they were satisfied with the type of work they do, which is somewhat higher than the overall percentage of officers who reported being satisfied with the type of work they do (75 per-

TABLE 8.1
Percentage of MHPs Satisfied or Very Satisfied with BHTs, Overall and by Service Branch

Satisfaction Domain	Overall $n = 654$	Army $n = 312$	Navy $n = 163$	Air Force $n = 179$
Satisfaction with type of work***	90.2	95.2[a]	80.0[b]	84.3[b]
Satisfaction with supervisor	69.0	70.2	61.3	71.1
Satisfaction with BHTs	57.0	55.7	56.5	60.6

NOTES: *** $p < 0.001$. Values with differing letter superscripts within rows are statistically different at the $p < 0.05$ level, according to post hoc paired comparisons.

cent) on the SOFS (U.S. Department of Defense, Office of People Analytics, 2017). There was a significant service branch difference, however, with Army MHPs reporting significantly higher satisfaction ($p < 0.05$). About 69 percent of MHPs reported being satisfied with the quality of their supervisor, compared with about 74 percent of the overall population of military officers (U.S. Department of Defense, Office of People Analytics, 2017).

In addition, we asked MHPs about their satisfaction with BHTs' performance. Again, response options ranged from "very dissatisfied" to "very satisfied." Nearly 60 percent of MHPs indicated that they were "satisfied" or "very satisfied" with the performance of BHTs (Table 8.1). In this section, we discuss MHPs' overall satisfaction (i.e., either "satisfied" or "very satisfied") with BHT performance and whether there were any significant differences in perceptions by service branch, military status, provider type, and the amount of time MHPs spent practicing in the MHS. Then, we assess the relationship between the proportion of MHPs who were satisfied with BHT performance and the proportion of MHPs who were supervisors, as well as the proportion of MHPs who believed that BHTs receive adequate supervision. Finally, we describe our analysis of the association between MHPs' satisfaction with BHT performance and their perceptions of BHTs' proficiency in performing clinical tasks.

Overall, about 26 percent of MHPs indicated that they were dissatisfied with BHTs' performance (Appendix Figure E.10), but there were no significant differences by service branch.

We examined whether there were associations between supervision-related factors and MHPs' satisfaction with the performance of BHTs (Figure 8.4). First, we found that a significantly greater proportion of MHPs who supervised BHTs (62 percent) were satisfied with BHTs' performance than MHPs who did not supervise BHTs (53 percent). MHPs who supervise BHTs likely have greater oversight and awareness of the tasks that BHTs perform, and they also feel more ownership over the performance of BHTs, possibly explaining why they were more likely to report that they were satisfied. Furthermore, we assessed the proportion of MHPs who indicated that they were satisfied with BHTs' performance based on whether they perceived that BHTs receive adequate supervision. MHPs who believed that BHTs receive adequate supervision were significantly more likely to indicate that they were satisfied with BHT performance (78 percent) than MHPs

FIGURE 8.4

MHP Satisfaction, by Supervision-Related Factors

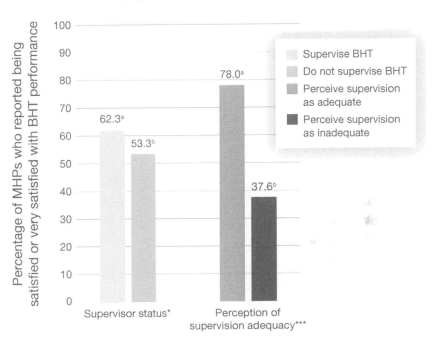

NOTES: *** $p < 0.001$. Values with differing letter superscripts within column clusters are statistically different at the $p < 0.05$ level, according to post hoc paired comparisons. Supervisor status: $n = 653$; perception of supervision adequacy: $n = 539$.

who did not perceive supervision to be adequate (38 percent). This finding highlights the key role of supervision in perceptions of BHT performance.

We examined variation in levels of MHP satisfaction with BHT performance based on several other factors, including military status, provider type, and the amount of time MHPs have spent practicing in the MHS, but we observed no significant differences.

As a final step, we examined whether satisfaction with BHT performance was associated with MHPs' perceptions of BHT proficiency in performing clinical tasks. There were significant correlations between the four subscores (screening/assessment, psychosocial intervention, treatment planning/monitoring, and outreach/resilience) and satisfaction with BHT performance (ranging from $r = 0.29$ for outreach/resilience to $r = 0.44$ for screening/assessment) ($p < 0.001$). This suggests that MHPs who perceive BHTs to be more proficient are also more satisfied with BHT performance.

BHTs' Fit for the Job

Finally, we examined the extent to which BHTs believed they were a good fit for their job. Two items were used to assess these perceptions: (1) "My personality is a good match for this job," and (2) "I am the right type of person for this type of work." Response options ranged from 1 (strongly disagree) to 7 (strongly agree).[1] In this section, we present BHTs' overall perceptions of their fit for their job and how that varied by BHTs' service branch, BHTs' reported levels of satisfaction with their military job, and BHTs' views on the quality of their supervisor. In addition, we describe the association between BHTs' reported person-job fit and their perceptions of the amount of time spent in various types of training. Finally, we analyze the correlation between BHTs' perceptions of person-job fit and their self-reported proficiency in performing clinical tasks, which might help explain a potential relationship between BHTs' level of confidence with their work and their sense of belonging in the BHT role.

About 70 percent of BHTs agreed or strongly agreed that their personality matched the BHT role and that they were the right type of person for this work. Average scores fell within the "somewhat agree" to "agree" range (Figure 8.5). By contrast, less than 10 percent of BHTs indicated that they disagreed that their personality fit their job or that they were the right type of person for this work (8 percent and 7 percent, respectively).

Figure 8.5 also provides the means of BHTs' responses by service branch in relation to BHTs' overall mean score. BHTs in the Air Force had significantly lower ratings of person-job fit across both items compared with Army and Navy BHTs. Air Force BHTs are required to complete the MMPI-2-RF, although how it is used is unclear. It may be that it is used to rule out candidates who are seen as unsuitable for the role (e.g., for personality or behavioral health reasons) rather than to identify those who are an optimal fit for the career field (Holliday et al., 2019).

---

[1] Responses on these items were highly correlated ($r = 0.83$, $p < 0.01$, $n = 524$).

FIGURE 8.5

Mean Ratings of Person-Job Fit, Overall and by Service Branch

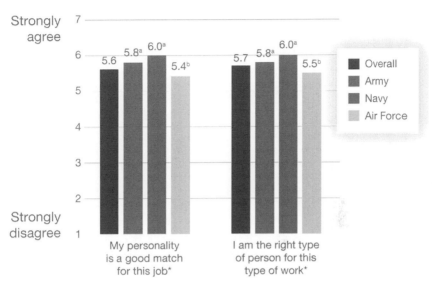

NOTES: * $p < 0.05$. Values with differing letter superscripts within column clusters are statistically different at the $p < 0.05$ level, according to post hoc paired comparisons. $n = 524$.

BHTs' ratings of their fit with the career field also varied significantly based on their reported levels of satisfaction with their military job (Figure 8.6) and their perceptions of the quality of their supervisor (Figure 8.7). Ratings of fit with the BHT career field were higher among BHTs who were satisfied with their military job. It may be that individuals who feel like this career field is a better match for their personality and skills are more satisfied with their work; however, it might also be that those who are satisfied with their work have developed a sense of belonging and higher level of comfort with their work.

We observed a similar association between BHT ratings of their fit with the career field and satisfaction with the quality of their supervisor. Across both items, mean ratings of person-job fit were highest among those who reported being satisfied with the quality of their supervisor. This is consistent with other research suggesting that higher person-job fit is associated with greater satisfaction (Lauver and Kristof-Brown, 2001). However, it also

FIGURE 8.6

Mean Ratings of Person-Job Fit, by BHT Satisfaction with Military Job

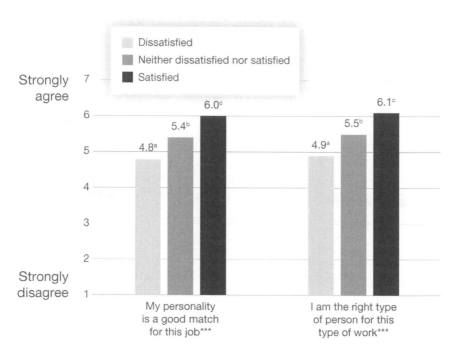

NOTES: *** $p < 0.001$. Values with differing letter superscripts within column clusters are statistically different at the $p < 0.05$ level, according to post hoc paired comparisons. $n = 524$.

might be that higher-quality supervision helps BHTs feel more confident or connected to their work.

We also assessed whether there was a relationship between each person-job fit item and BHTs' perceptions of the amount of time spent in various types of training, but we observed no significant associations. Furthermore, there was no significant association between BHTs' perceptions of their person-job fit and their perceptions of adequacy of supervision. This suggests that training does not necessarily drive perceptions of fit with the career field. Rather, it might be that fit with the BHT role is more a factor of personality and that this, in turn, contributes to higher satisfaction in the role.

FIGURE 8.7

Ratings of Person-Job Fit, by BHT Satisfaction with Quality of Supervisor

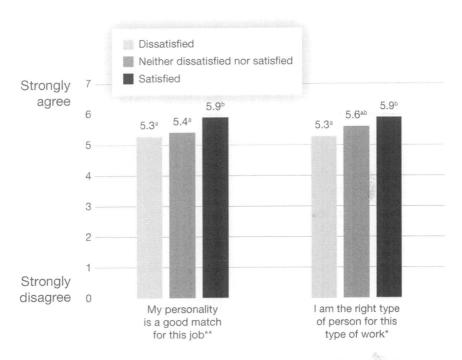

NOTES: ** $p < 0.01$, * $p < 0.05$. Values with differing letter superscripts within column clusters are statistically different at the $p < 0.05$ level, according to post hoc paired comparisons. $n = 524$.

As a final analysis, we examined whether perceptions of person-job fit were associated with BHT-reported proficiency in performing clinical tasks, for which we used the subscores described in Chapter Four (proficiency for screening/assessment, psychosocial intervention, treatment planning/ monitoring, and outreach/resilience). BHTs' ratings of whether their personality was a match for the job were significantly associated with their self-reported proficiency to perform psychosocial interventions ($r = 0.16$, $p < 0.001$) and outreach/resilience tasks ($r = 0.10$, $p < 0.05$). BHTs' ratings of whether they were the right type of person for the work were significantly associated with self-reported proficiency for each type of task. Correlations ranged from $r = 0.13$ for screening/assessment ($p < 0.01$) to $r = 0.19$ for psychosocial interventions ($p < 0.001$).

Summary

About two-thirds of BHTs reported that they were satisfied or very satisfied with their work and with the quality of their supervisor. This is similar to the overall proportion of enlisted service members who reported being satisfied with their work and supervisor in the annual SOFS, suggesting that BHTs are at least as satisfied as enlisted personnel in other career fields. However, significantly fewer Air Force BHTs reported that they were satisfied with their work than their Army counterparts. This was somewhat surprising, particularly because our findings described in other chapters of this report suggest that Air Force BHTs engage more frequently in clinical activities, report higher levels of proficiency in performing clinical tasks, and indicate that their training is more sufficient than that received by BHTs in other service branches. In addition, about 64 percent of enlisted Air Force service members who responded to the SOFS reported that they are satisfied with their work, compared to 57 percent of Air Force BHTs who participated in our survey. It is unclear what accounts for this relatively lower level of satisfaction.

Our findings also suggest that the nature of BHT responsibilities contributes to their satisfaction. BHTs who spent more time in clinical care were more likely to report that they were satisfied with their work, and those who spent more time on each type of clinical task (screening/assessment, psychosocial intervention, treatment planning/monitoring, and outreach/resilience) were more satisfied. It appears that when BHTs spend more time on clinical tasks—rather than administrative responsibilities or unit responsibilities—they are more satisfied with their work. In addition, BHTs who were more confident in their ability to perform clinical tasks were more satisfied with their work. There may be times that clinic or unit demands require that BHTs spend time on nonclinical tasks. However, these findings suggest that clinics should work to ensure that BHTs have opportunities to perform clinical tasks to the extent possible.

We also assessed MHP satisfaction with BHTs' performance. About 57 percent of MHPs indicated that they were satisfied, and there were no significant differences by service branch. We found that MHPs who supervised BHTs were more satisfied with BHTs' performance, as were those who believed that BHTs received enough supervision. This further highlights the importance of supervision. Not only are BHTs more satisfied when they receive adequate supervision, but MHPs are also more satisfied and, in turn, perhaps more likely to integrate BHTs into clinical tasks.

Finally, we examined the extent to which BHTs believed they are a fit for the career field. We found that most BHTs believed their personality is a good match for the BHT role and that they are the right type of person for the work. Less than 10 percent of BHTs indicated that they were not a good match for the role. In addition, BHTs who indicated that they were not a strong fit for the job were less satisfied with the work and the quality of their supervision. This raises important questions as to whether these individuals are less likely to be comfortable with their work, or even less motivated to develop their skills through continuing education or OJT. Of note, BHT perceptions of their training were not associated with ratings of person-job fit. This suggests that training is not enough to overcome perceptions that the BHT career field is not a good match. It is important to consider whether there are additional selection procedures that could be put in place to assess fit with the BHT role. The potential importance of such screening measures is underscored by our finding that BHTs who indicated that they were a good match for this career field felt more confident performing clinical tasks. Although confidence is not necessarily a proxy for skill level, these results suggest that perceptions of fit with the role might affect how BHTs approach their day-to-day work.

CHAPTER NINE

Perceptions of Changes to BHT Practice

In this chapter, we examine potential changes to BHT practice or how MHPs integrate these personnel into clinical settings with the goal of identifying how BHTs could contribute more effectively to providing high-quality behavioral health care to service members across the MHS. Whereas Chapter Seven provided insights into the barriers that might prevent BHTs from being integrated into clinical settings, this chapter identifies potential policy and practice solutions.

BHT Perspectives of Changes to BHT Practice

To gain a better sense of how BHTs can be most effectively integrated into the behavioral health workforce, we presented survey respondents with a series of statements regarding potential changes to BHT practice. BHTs and MHPs reported the extent to which they agreed that each option would enable BHTs to contribute more effectively across the MHS. Response options were "not at all," "slightly," "moderately," "very much," and "extremely." In this section, we explore the types of solutions that BHTs felt would be most useful for their work and analyze whether there were any significant differences by service branch and time in practice as a BHT.

Figure 9.1 summarizes the percentage of BHTs who endorsed "very much" or "extremely" for each potential change in BHT practice. Most strikingly, the vast majority of BHTs believed that BHTs should be provided with ongoing professional development opportunities (90 percent). This finding is consistent with the results presented in previous chapters, par-

FIGURE 9.1

Percentage of BHTs Who Agreed Very Much or Extremely with Potential Changes

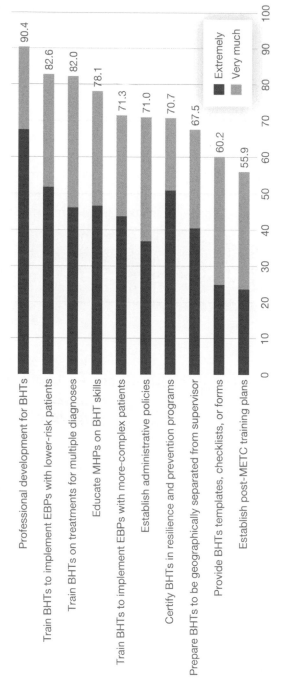

NOTE: *n* = 524–525.

ticularly regarding variability in skills. BHTs also indicated that they could be more effective if they received training to implement approaches that are effective across multiple psychiatric diagnoses and to provide EBPs to lower-risk patients.

Only a small proportion of BHTs endorsed "not at all" or "slightly" for each of the proposed changes (Figure E.11 in Appendix E). However, there were two potential solutions in particular that BHTs did not favor. About 15 percent of BHTs indicated that establishing specific training plans for BHTs upon leaving METC or preparing BHTs to work in geographic locations where they are physically separated from their supervisor would not be very effective. It might be that scenarios in which a BHT would need to work in geographic locations separate from their supervising provider are rare and therefore would have little impact in practice. However, it might also be that BHTs felt less comfortable with this option.

We also conducted analyses to evaluate whether there were differences in endorsing each potential change across service branches or time in practice as a BHT. We provide an overview of findings here, and complete tables of results can be found in Appendix E. There were few differences in the proportions of BHTs who endorsed each potential change in BHT practice by service branch (Table E.7 in Appendix E), although the top potential changes varied slightly. BHTs across all service branches most commonly indicated that the provision of opportunities for professional development would be effective. BHTs in the Army and Navy BHTs indicated that training BHTs to use EBPs with lower-risk patients would be the next most-useful change to BHT practice (81 percent and 91 percent, respectively), followed by training for BHTs to implement approaches that are effective across multiple psychiatric diagnoses (80 percent and 88 percent, respectively). Air Force BHTs' second and third most highly endorsed changes were the same as those of Army and Navy BHTs but in reverse order. In addition, Air Force BHTs were less likely to indicate that it would be effective to have BHTs become certified trainers for resilience-oriented programs outside the MHS, perhaps because fewer Air Force BHTs work in embedded behavioral health positions.

Because BHTs at different career stages might have different roles and responsibilities, we examined perceptions of each potential change based on how long a BHT has spent in practice, finding only minor differences by years in practice (Table E.8 in Appendix E).

MHP Perspectives on Changes to BHT Practice

MHPs were also asked to indicate their perceptions of the extent to which each potential change to BHT practice would enable them to be more effective in the MHS, using the same scale of "not at all" to "extremely." In this section, we examine MHPs' views on these proposed changes, as well as whether certain types of MHPs support these changes based on their service branch, time in practice in the MHS, military status, or provider type.

Similar to BHTs, the most commonly endorsed change was to provide BHTs with opportunities to participate in ongoing professional development (78 percent; Figure 9.2). Other commonly endorsed changes included providing education to MHPs on how best to integrate BHTs into clinical settings and establishing administrative policies to better define components of BHT work. This suggests a need to establish a common understanding of BHTs' roles and responsibilities. In addition, about two-thirds of MHPs indicated that BHTs should be trained to implement treatment approaches that are effective across diagnoses and be provided with forms that could be used to structure clinical tasks. Training BHTs in trans-diagnostic approaches has the potential to maximize the types of patients that a BHT could see, while clinical support tools might help MHPs feel more comfortable entrusting a task to a BHT.

Our findings indicate that BHTs and MHPs share common views regarding the need for BHTs to continue to grow their skills and knowledge base beyond their training at METC. However, unlike BHTs, more than 50 percent of MHPs (51.3 percent) reported that training BHTs to implement EBPs with more-complex patients would only be "slightly" or "not at all" useful (Figure E.12 in Appendix E). This could reflect a preference on the part of MHPs for more complex patients to be seen by credentialed providers, but it could also reflect concerns about the current training or skill level of BHTs.

We also conducted analyses to evaluate whether differences in endorsing each potential change existed across service branches, or by time in practice in the MHS, military status, or provider type. We provide an

FIGURE 9.2

Percentage of MHPs Who Agreed Very Much or Extremely with Potential Changes

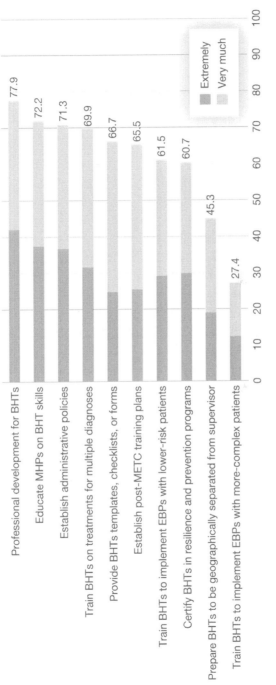

NOTE: n = 653–656.

overview of findings here, and complete tables of results can be found in Appendix E. We observed only slight differences in the top three potential changes to BHT practice by service branch (Table E.9 in Appendix E). The most frequently endorsed statement, regardless of service branch, remained "Provide BHTs ongoing opportunities for professional development." The second most commonly supported change endorsed by Army and Navy MHPs was establishing administrative policies to better define components of BHT work, followed by educating MHPs on how they can utilize BHTs. The remaining top two changes endorsed by Air Force MHPs were that MHPs should be provided with education about how to utilize BHTs, but also that BHTs ought to be trained to implement treatment approaches that are effective across multiple psychiatric diagnoses.

We also examined whether there was variation in perceptions about potential changes based on how long an MHP had practiced in the MHS. Although there was some variability by time in practice, these differences were largely not significant (Appendix Table E.10). However, MHPs with more than 20 years of experience in the MHS were significantly less likely to endorse training BHTs to implement treatment approaches that are effective across multiple psychiatric diagnoses or training BHTs to implement EBPs with lower-risk patients. This finding might reflect a recent shift in the role of BHTs to be more integrated into clinical care, and more-tenured MHPs who might not yet be comfortable with BHTs having these responsibilities. Furthermore, MHPs who had been practicing for more than 20 years were also less supportive of establishing administrative policies to better define components of BHT work.

Active-duty and civilian MHPs differed in regard to some of their per-ceptions of potential changes to BHT practice (Table E.11 in Appendix E). For example, active-duty MHPs were more likely to endorse training BHTs to implement treatment approaches that are effective across multiple psy-chiatric diagnoses, training BHTs to implement EBPs with lower-risk patients, and preparing BHTs to work in geographic locations where they are physically separated from their supervising provider. It is possible that active-duty providers have a better sense of BHTs' role in deployed settings because of their military background and are more willing to utilize BHTs for treatment-related tasks as a way to develop their skills.

We also explored any potential differences in perceptions of changes to BHT practice by provider type (Table E.12 in Appendix E). Although only a small proportion of MHPs overall endorsed training BHTs to implement EBPs with more-complex patients, doctoral-level psychologists were least likely to endorse this solution (17 percent) compared to psychiatrists or psychiatric nurse practitioners (27 percent) and master's-level clinicians (33 percent) ($p < 0.05$).

BHT and MHP Agreement on Potential Changes to BHT Practice

We compared the percentage of BHTs and MHPs who endorsed each of the potential changes to BHT practice to identify those with the highest agreement, as well as the largest discrepancies. There was less than a 1-percent difference in the proportion of BHTs and MHPs who indicated that establishing administrative policies to better define BHT work would be useful (Figure 9.3). A similar proportion of BHTs and MHPs also indicated that educating MHPs on how to use BHTs and providing templates, checklists, or forms to structure clinical tasks would enable BHTs to be more effective within the MHS. Because a large proportion of both groups see the benefits of these types of policy changes, these may both be effective and garner buy-in from both BHTs and MHPs. Although MHPs ranked these three changes within their top five adjustments to BHT practice, only the recommendation to provide education to MHPs on how they can utilize BHTs fell within BHTs' top five changes.

We also assessed the largest discrepancies in BHT and MHP responses (Figure 9.4). The largest difference was observed for training BHTs to implement EBPs with clinically complex patients (43.9 percent difference), which was endorsed as potentially effective by a much larger proportion of BHTs than MHPs. Results presented in Chapter Four indicated that both BHTs and MHPs reported that BHTs do not currently administer EBPs very often, which may partially explain why fewer MHPs may find this change in BHT practice less essential than BHTs, who may want further training in this area. This might also be indicative of a more fundamental difference in the ways the BHTs and MHPs perceive the responsibilities of BHTs. For

FIGURE 9.3

Potential Changes to BHT Practice with Highest Agreement Between BHTs and MHPs

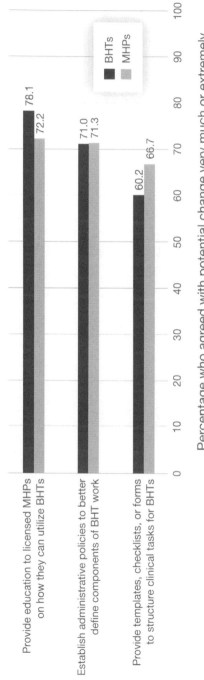

Percentage who agreed with potential change very much or extremely

NOTES: BHTs: *n* = 525; MHPs: *n* = 654–656.

FIGURE 9.4

Potential Changes to BHT Practice with Largest Discrepancies Between BHTs and MHPs

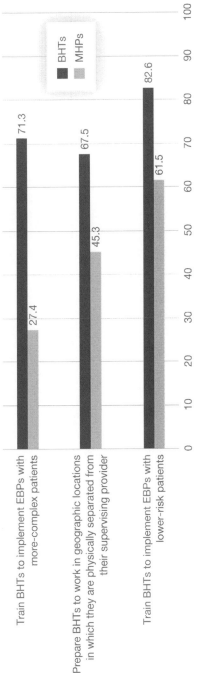

NOTES: BHTs: $n = 524$; MHPs: $n = 653$–654.

example, MHPs may feel uncomfortable allowing BHTs to take on more complex patients, even with additional training.

There was also about a 20-percent difference in the proportion of BHTs and MHPs who endorsed the need to prepare BHTs to work in geographic locations physically separated from their supervising provider and training BHTs to implement EBPs with lower-risk patients. In general, it appears that BHTs are interested in changes to practice that allow them more autonomy, whereas MHPs do not tend to favor these solutions. This may reflect the fact that many MHPs indicated that BHTs were not proficient when performing more routine tasks, such as triaging patients and conducting risk assessments.

As a final step to understanding the concordance between BHT and MHP perceptions of these potential changes to practice, we conducted a Spearman rank correlation test. Results indicated that there was not a statistically significant correlation ($r = 0.33$).

Summary

This chapter examined BHT and MHP perceptions of changes to policy, training, and practice that would enable BHTs to be more effective within the MHS. Both BHTs and MHPs agreed that BHTs would benefit from opportunities to participate in ongoing professional development (e.g., courses through Army Medical Department Center and School, obtaining civilian credentials). This is unsurprising, given that substantial proportions of BHTs and MHPs indicated that BHTs spend insufficient time on OJT and continuing education (as reported in Chapter Six). There may be some obstacles to providing additional training. For example, BHTs are already tasked with balancing clinical, administrative, and unit responsibilities. However, these findings suggest the importance of finding ways to carve out additional training time, or perhaps establishing more concrete guidance regarding time spent on professional development activities.

Many BHTs and MHPs also indicated that MHPs would benefit from education on the best way to integrate BHTs into the MHS. This type of guidance could include information about the basic skills of BHTs who leave METC; the range of clinical activities they might assist with, as well as expectations regarding time spent in clinical activities; and recommendations for supervision and OJT. One example of such an effort is the *Healthcare Provider's Practice Guide for the Utilization of Behavioral Health Technicians (BHTs)*, a document developed by the BHTWG that addresses many of these themes (Defense Health Agency, 2019). In addition, many MHPs indicated that it would be useful to establish administrative policies to better define components of BHTs' work (e.g., expectations for roles, supervision). This type of policy document might serve as another useful guide for MHPs.

Some potential changes related to training BHTs to have a greater role in delivering psychosocial interventions, including clinical approaches that are effective across multiple diagnoses and EBP for both low-risk patients and those with complex needs. Both BHTs and MHPs indicated the potential utility of training BHTs in approaches that are effective across diagnoses, such as problem-solving therapy. However, relatively fewer MHPs than BHTs indicated that BHTs should be trained to implement EBPs with lower-risk patients (e.g., cognitive behavioral therapy for depression), and only about one-quarter of MHPs reported that BHTs should do so for complex patients (e.g., cognitive processing therapy for PTSD). These findings suggest that BHTs are interested in providing psychosocial interventions. However, MHPs might believe that BHTs are better suited to providing treatment to higher-functioning individuals, even with additional training. That said, active-duty MHPs appeared to be more open to BHTs providing EBPs to lower-risk patients, which may reflect an understanding of the expanded role of BHTs in deployed settings.

MHPs also reported that it would be effective to provide BHTs with templates, checklists, or forms to structure clinical tasks (e.g., clinical interviews). These types of clinical support tools might increase MHP confidence that BHTs are covering needed topics during their clinical encounters, especially when working with a BHT who completed training more recently.

BHTs and MHPs appeared to be split in their perceptions of preparing BHTs to work in geographic locations in which they are physically separated from their supervising provider (e.g., receiving video or electronic supervision). BHTs in practice for more than seven years were especially likely to endorse this item, as were active-duty MHPs. It may be that these BHTs and MHPs were more aware of the demands of BHTs in certain operational settings and understood that, although this type of supervision arrangement is not common, there are certain situations in which it is mission-critical.

CHAPTER TEN

Conclusions and Recommendations

This report described BHT and MHP perspectives on the roles of BHTs in the MHS and embedded settings. This included the tasks BHTs complete most often, BHT and MHP perspectives on BHT proficiency, and perceptions of the adequacy of BHT training and supervision. We also examined potential barriers affecting BHT involvement in clinical tasks, BHT satisfaction and fit with the career field, and potential changes that would improve the integration of BHTs into the MHS. In this chapter, we discuss the strengths and limitations of our analysis, summarize our findings, and present policy recommendations and directions for future research.

Strengths and Limitations

This study had several significant strengths. First, this was a large, comprehensive survey of BHTs—perhaps the largest survey of BHTs ever conducted. A small amount of research literature has focused on the role of BHTs, but those studies have tended to be conceptual or have utilized small samples, and their findings were often specific to a single service branch. This has historically limited the generalizability of research recommendations. By contrast, our study reached BHTs across the U.S. military, and our sample varied in its demographic characteristics, rank, and time in service. Combined with the large sample size, this allowed us to explore variability on key outcomes by service branch and other BHT characteristics.

Second, our surveys covered a wide range of domains. We examined the frequency with which BHTs performed clinical tasks, perceptions of BHT proficiency in performing those tasks, BHT satisfaction with their work and fit with the career field, and MHP satisfaction with BHTs' work. Previous research has highlighted potential barriers to integrating BHTs into clinical tasks, but our survey allowed us to evaluate the extent to which BHTs and MHPs agree on these barriers. Finally, because we posed parallel sets of questions to BHTs and MHPs, we were able to formally compare their perspectives and identify areas of agreement and disagreement. Areas of disagreement provided insight into potential weaknesses in how BHT roles have been defined and additional training needs. At the same time, areas of agreement provided insight into potential opportunities for more effectively integrating BHTs into the MHS.

This study also had certain limitations. First, our survey sample and contact information were drawn from the DMDC. Although these data are updated annually, there were likely some individuals for whom we did not have up-to-date contact information. In addition, our adjusted response rate was 42 percent for BHTs and 37 percent for MHPs—rates comparable to those in previous surveys of providers (Hepner et al., 2017). These factors could affect the representativeness of our sample. However, we performed weighted analyses to help ensure the representativeness of our findings.

Second, only a small proportion of BHTs (3.7 percent) were deployed at the time of our survey. Therefore, we did not have adequate statistical power to examine differences in the frequency of BHT tasks or BHT-reported proficiency for tasks by deployment status. To address this, we included a set of questions for any BHT who deployed in the previous 12 months to examine differences in the frequency of each broad category of tasks (i.e., screening/assessment, psychosocial intervention, treatment planning and monitoring, and outreach and resilience). However, these questions provided less nuance on the extent to which the frequency of these tasks changes in deployed settings compared to garrison MTFs. Finally, our survey was conducted during the COVID-19 pandemic, when behavioral health care delivery in the MHS was markedly disrupted. At the same time, BHTs were asked to provide support for COVID-19 preparedness efforts (Frampton, 2020; Thomas, 2020), such as conducting symptom screening and patient outreach.

Key Findings

The results of our analyses highlighted the following key findings.

There Can Be Substantial Variability in BHT Responsibilities and Skills, Including Time Spent on Clinical Tasks

Our findings indicate that BHTs engage in a wide variety of tasks, including screening and assessment, psychosocial interventions, treatment planning and monitoring, and outreach and resilience activities. Both BHTs and MHPs reported that BHTs perform screening and assessment activities most often, yet there was some variation in the amount of time BHTs spent on other clinical tasks, depending on their branch of service and current assignment. For example, Air Force BHTs appear to engage in certain types of tasks more often than BHTs in other service branches. Moreover, about half of BHTs who had deployed in the 12 months prior to our survey indicated that they performed more screening and assessment tasks, psychosocial interventions, and outreach and resilience tasks—and fewer treatment planning/monitoring activities—while serving in a deployed setting. Furthermore, about 90 percent of BHTs and MHPs indicated that there can be substantial variability in BHT skills, even within the same rank. This finding reinforces that there is a broad range of BHT skills and suggests that not all BHTs have the same opportunity for ongoing training to maintain and develop their skills.

Our findings indicated that, on average, BHTs spent about one-third of their time in an average week on patient care–related responsibilities, although this varied significantly across service branches. The remainder of their time was split between administrative clinic responsibilities, non-clinical responsibilities, and other tasks, such as training or management responsibilities. A substantial proportion of BHTs (62 percent) agreed that BHTs are primarily needed to cover the administrative needs in clinics, which might serve as a barrier to integrating them into clinical care. However, only 39 percent of MHPs agreed with this same barrier, suggesting differing views of the BHT role.

In turn, the variability in BHTs' tasks means that BHTs might not get the opportunity to perform certain tasks very often. As a result, BHTs might have less experience and proficiency with some tasks than others, and they might find themselves unprepared when they change settings or assignments. This has additional implications, particularly for patient care activities, when BHTs are deployed and may be tasked with performing certain activities for which they are not fully prepared. In addition, although administrative tasks seem to be a common part of the BHT role, we found that BHTs reported greater satisfaction with their work when they spent more time performing patient care–related activities, which could affect their engagement with their work or their longevity in the career field.

BHTs and MHPs Differed in Their Perceptions of BHT Proficiency

Our findings revealed that although BHTs and MHPs generally agreed that BHTs are most proficient at screening and assessment-related tasks, BHTs perceived themselves to be more proficient in performing these tasks. For example, 97 percent of BHTs perceived themselves to be proficient in conducting risk assessments, compared with 43 percent of MHPs. We observed significant discrepancies between BHT- and MHP-reported proficiency across all clinical tasks assessed. One potential explanation is that BHTs were unaware of their weaknesses on certain tasks. However, it may also be that MHPs had unrealistic expectations for BHTs' skills.

More than two-thirds of MHPs and almost 60 percent of BHTs agreed or strongly agreed with the statement, "Licensed mental health providers are not familiar with the range of clinical activities behavioral health technicians are trained to provide." These findings underscore the lack of clarity among MHPs regarding the skills that BHTs possess and emphasize the need for greater education for MHPs regarding the role of BHTs. In fact, more than three-quarters of MHPs indicated that education about how best to utilize BHTs' skills could improve the effectiveness of BHTs in the MHS.

The misalignment in BHT and MHP perceptions likely affects the way BHTs are integrated into clinical settings. MHPs who are not confident in BHT skills might feel more comfortable tasking BHTs with administrative responsibilities. In addition, we found that MHPs' satisfaction with BHTs' performance was significantly associated with MHPs' perceptions of BHT proficiency. MHPs who have had a positive experience with BHTs might be more likely to integrate them more meaningfully into clinical tasks.

BHTs and MHPs Perceived Opportunities to Improve BHT Training, Including Continuing Education and Supervision

Both BHTs and MHPs reported that BHTs spend insufficient time engaging in ongoing training opportunities, but MHPs especially expressed concerns about time spent in training. For instance, while roughly a third of BHTs reported not spending enough time in OJT, nearly 56 percent of MHPs felt similarly. MHPs who supervised BHTs appeared particularly concerned about the amount of continuing education that BHTs receive. There were some differences by branch of service; for example, Air Force BHTs and MHPs were least likely to indicate that the amount of time spent on continuing education was inadequate compared with their Army and Navy counterparts. This could reflect, in part, the Air Force's well-standardized continuing education requirements for BHT career progression, which could be used as a potential model for the other services.

There also appear to be opportunities to improve supervision practices. About 40 percent of MHPs reported that BHTs did not receive enough supervision, and about 16 percent indicated that they were unsure whether supervision was adequate. Although a smaller proportion of BHTs reported that supervision was inadequate, they did indicate that MHPs had limited time for supervision. MHPs also acknowledged that they had limited time for supervision, and many reported that BHTs could benefit from more-systematic supervision. Of note, BHTs who indicated that they received inadequate supervision reported being less satisfied with their work and their supervisor. Therefore, improvements to BHT supervision might also improve BHT effectiveness and satisfaction.

Recommendations

We identified four recommendations to optimize the role of BHTs. These recommendations focus on identifying opportunities to reduce variability in BHT skills, as well as improving ongoing training and supervision for BHTs.

Recommendation 1. Standardize Expectations for BHTs' Scope of Practice and Educate Providers on BHT Roles

Our findings make it clear that BHTs can play a wide variety of roles. In many ways, this is by design: BHT technical training covers a broad range of clinical topics and skills, and service branch policies outline a broad range of BHT responsibilities. However, this means that BHTs might be asked to perform different tasks depending on their setting and supervisor, which can lead to uneven skill development. This could partially explain the large proportion of BHTs and MHPs who raised concerns about variability in BHT skills, even within the same rank.

One way to address this issue would be to standardize expectations for BHTs' scope of practice. This might include specific guidelines about skills that BHTs are expected to maintain regardless of setting and could focus on high-frequency tasks, such as performing risk assessments, completing intake interviews, and administering and scoring behavioral health symptom measures. At the same time, it could also make clear any tasks that BHTs should not be expected to perform. For example, many of the responses to the question about out-of-scope BHT tasks related to the provision of psychotherapy or work with high-acuity patients. BHTs might not be fully prepared to take on these tasks because EBP for mental health and substance use concerns appear to be low-frequency tasks for BHTs. In turn, such standardized expectations lend themselves to the development of competency assessment mechanisms to ensure that BHTs develop and maintain the requisite skills. Efforts to standardize the role of BHTs could focus not just on the range of clinical activities BHTs might perform but also on the time BHTs spend on administrative and nonclinical tasks. Limited time spent on patient care can hamper skill development, and it might also reduce satisfaction with the role.

The service branches have their own policy documents describing BHTs' scope of practice. However, as oversight of health care delivery by the Defense Health Agency leads to increased standardization in practice, a standard scope of practice that applies across services branches might reduce between-service variability in skill development. This could especially advantageous for BHTs working in joint MTFs, where the other behavioral health staff may be from different services. In these settings, a shared understanding of the BHT role will ensure these personnel are meaningfully integrated into workflows.

In addition to standardizing the role of BHTs, it is important that MHPs know what BHTs can do and are expected to do. Nearly three-quarters of MHPs indicated that educating MHPs on BHT skills would increase BHTs' effectiveness in the MHS. There have already been efforts to do so. For example, in 2019, the BHTWG published the *Healthcare Provider's Practice Guide for the Utilization of Behavioral Health Technicians* (Defense Health Agency, 2019). The guide includes a broad overview of BHT technical training and OJT requirements, then details the types of roles that BHTs could play in clinical care, embedded roles, and roles in deployed settings. There is also an overview of supervision requirements and types of supervision. Codifying expectations for BHTs in administrative policies could help reduce variability in practice and provide a reference for MHPs. About 71 percent of BHTs and MHPs favored establishing administrative policies to better define components of BHTs' work.

Recommendation 2. Provide Clinical Support Tools to Structure BHT Tasks

Our findings highlighted discrepancies between BHT and MHP perspectives on BHT proficiency across clinical tasks. Clinical support tools might be one way to address this issue. About two-thirds of MHPs said that providing templates, checklists, or forms to structure clinical tasks would be an effective strategy for integrating BHTs into the MHS. These support tools could focus on the tasks that BHTs perform most frequently, such as screening and assessment. Focusing on tasks with large discrepancies between BHT and MHP perceptions, including performing risk assessments, might also be especially effective. For example, BHTs could be trained to use a standardized interview form to ensure that they collect all relevant information for a risk assessment. This type of template could include decision support as to when the BHT should engage an MHP to see the patient. These types of clinical support tools could improve the quality of the clinical encounter and increase MHP confidence in integrating BHTs into certain tasks.

Clinical support tools could be developed to structure other types of clinical tasks. For example, 70 percent of MHPs and 82 percent of BHTs indicated that it could be effective to train BHTs to implement treatment approaches that are effective across multiple psychiatric diagnoses. As suggested in our prior report, this could include manualized or structured interventions that have been adapted for non-MHP mental health personnel, such as problem-solving therapy or motivational enhancement therapy (Holliday et al., 2019). Our findings suggest that training BHTs to implement these types of transdiagnostic approaches or deliver EBPs to lower-risk patients is more likely to garner buy-in from MHPs than training BHTs to implement evidence-based psychotherapies for more-complex patients. Lessons on how to train BHTs to implement EBPs can be drawn from the mental health task–shifting literature, which addresses training for non–mental health professionals to perform psychological interventions. For example, materials to guide sessions (e.g., worksheets or handouts) can be effective, although adequate supervision remains a key component (Shahmalak et al., 2019).

The MHS is already beginning to explore how such tools could be implemented in clinical settings. PHCoE has initiated an effort to develop a clinical support tool for BHTs and has previously released these types of clinical support tools for other topics, including management of major depressive disorder and safety planning with patients at risk for suicide (U.S. Department of Defense and U.S. Department of Veterans Affairs, 2020), which include decision algorithms, fact sheets, and assessment guides.

Recommendation 3. Standardize and Communicate Expectations for Supervision Through Policy Guidance

Our findings highlighted a need to improve current supervision practices for BHTs. Seventy-eight percent of MHPs indicated a need for more-structured supervision of BHTs, while 66 percent of BHTs indicated that MHPs have limited time to invest in supervision and training. BHTs who spend limited time on patient care might especially be in need of supervision to develop their skills. This challenge could reflect a lack of specificity in requirements related to supervision of BHTs. As we previously found, supervision can include a wide variety of activities, including direct observation of work, cofacilitating sessions, and staffing cases after BHTs provide one-on-one services. There has also been little specificity as to the amount of time BHTs should spend being supervised by MHPs. However, more-standardized supervision has important benefits for skill development and might also facilitate the implementation of more-formalized competency assessments.

As health care services are integrated under the Defense Health Agency, there will be opportunities to create policies related to supervision. This could include standards for the amount of supervision each week and what modalities qualify as formal supervision (versus informal consultation). Such documents should also address potential changes to supervision in deployed environments, when BHTs might be expected to operate more autonomously and sometimes when geographically separated from their supervising provider.

Recommendation 4. Expand Continuing Education for BHTs, Such as Through the Development of a BHT-Specific Continuing Education Curriculum

The initial BHT technical training curriculum covers a wide range of topics, but the brief duration of training limits the amount of depth with which any given topic can be covered. However, only a small proportion of BHTs and MHPs indicated that METC training was inadequate. By comparison, 55 percent of BHTs and 69 percent of MHPs reported that BHTs spend too little time on continuing education. This likely reflects, at least in part, the understanding that METC is designed to provide a foundation of knowledge and skills. Although a substantial proportion of BHTs and MHPs also indicated that not enough time is spent on the clinical practicum experience that is part of training at METC, expanding this component might not be practical because of the staffing levels needed to provide supervision while BHTs are at military and community practicum sites. Furthermore, expanded time in practicum might not be sufficient to have a continued impact over the course of a BHT's career. It is in part for this reason that skill development is expected to continue through OJT and continuing education.

Air Force BHTs and MHPs were less likely to indicate that there was too little time spent on continuing education. This might be because the Air Force has a more-standardized continuing education curriculum. As part of their progression in their career field, Air Force BHTs must complete specific career development courses via home-study (U.S. Air Force, 2015; Headquarters U.S. Air Force, 2019). The creation of standardized continuing education curriculum is beneficial because it ensures that all BHTs receive education on the same topics. The implementation of these types of requirements could be a useful model for continuing professional development across all service branches. At a basic level, the specific content of the continuing education courses could be guided by the tasks BHTs perform most frequently or the types of presenting concerns they see most frequently in clinical settings. In addition, if efforts were made to standardize the BHT role or train them on certain evidence-based practices, these tasks could be the focus of continuing education courses.

Summary

This report presented the results of a novel investigation into the role of BHTs in the military. Consistent with how their roles are described in policy documents across service branches, our results demonstrated that BHTs are currently integrated into a wide range of clinical tasks. However, our findings also highlighted opportunities to optimize their role by standardizing expectations, providing additional clinical tools, and enhancing the training and supervision they receive. In addition to improving the satisfaction of BHTs and the MHPs who work with BHTs, these efforts have the potential to maximize the impact of the BHT role, which has implications for the efficiency and effectiveness of the MHS and for behavioral health care quality and readiness across the force.

Survey Sampling and Weighting

This appendix provides details on the sampling and weighting procedures summarized in Chapter Two.

Survey Sampling

Sampling Frame

Tables A.1 and A.2 provide details about the sampling frame of BHTs and MHPs, respectively. Table A.1 provides the number of BHTs in strata defined by service branch. Service branch is the only level of stratification we employ in our stratified sampling of BHTs. Table A.2 provides the number of MHPs in strata defined by service branch (Army, Navy, and Air Force), military status (active-duty versus civilian), and provider type (psychiatrist, nurse practitioner, doctoral psychologist, master's-level psychologists, and social workers). In all, we sampled independently from 30 substrata for MHPs, defined by three service branches, two military statuses, and five provider types.

Sampling Rates

We sampled from the populations described in Tables A.1 and A.2 at rates defined in Tables A.3 and A.4, respectively. The sampling rates detailed in

TABLE A.1
Number of BHTs, by Service Branch

Active-Duty Service Members	Army	Navy	Air Force	Total
BHT	1,148	231	857	2,236

TABLE A.2

Number of MHPs in the Provider Population, by Stratum

Active-Duty Service Member	Army	Navy	Air Force	Total
Psychiatrist	210	167	141	518
Psychiatric nurse practitioner	70	34	46	150
Psychologist (doctoral-level)	171	143	142	456
Psychologist (master's-level)	57	7	75	139
Social worker	323	81	274	678
Total	831	432	678	1,941
Civilian	**Army**	**Navy**	**Air Force**	**Total**
Psychiatrist	112	42	7	161
Psychiatric nurse practitioner	6	14	0	20
Psychologist (doctoral-level)	498	124	42	664
Psychologist (master's-level)	194	26	2	222
Social worker	1,193	170	279	1,642
Total	2,003	376	330	2,709
Total (active-duty and civilian providers)	**Army**	**Navy**	**Air Force**	**Total**
Psychiatrist	322	209	148	679
Psychiatric nurse practitioner	76	48	46	170
Psychologist (doctoral-level)	669	267	184	1,120
Psychologist (master's-level)	251	33	77	361
Social worker	1,516	251	553	2,320
Total	2,834	808	1,008	4,650

Tables A.3 and A.4 were determined to provide statistical power to detect small-to-medium effect sizes in comparisons between pre-defined substrata. For BHTs, sampling proportions were determined to power the three substrata defined by service branch. Note that we sampled all Navy BHTs because of their comparatively small population size.

For MHPs, we chose to power comparisons between substrata defined by service branch or provider type. We did not attempt to power any substrata defined by military status even though we sampled these substrata inde-

TABLE A.3
Proportion of BHTs Sampled from Each Service Branch

Active-Duty Service Member	Army	Navy	Air Force	Total
BHT (%)	47.0	100.0	63.0	58.6

TABLE A.4
Proportion of MHPs Sampled from Each Stratum

Active-Duty Service Member (%)	Army	Navy	Air Force	Total
Psychiatrist	70.0	70.1	92.2	76.1
Psychiatric nurse practitioner	100.0	100.0	100.0	100.0
Psychologist (doctoral-level)	36.3	46.9	69.7	50.0
Psychologist (master's-level)	17.5	57.1	22.7	22.3
Social worker	17.0	51.9	23.0	23.6
Total	41.4	61.1	52.4	49.6
Civilian (%)	Army	Navy	Air Force	Total
Psychiatrist	89.3	88.1	100.0	89.4
Psychiatric nurse practitioner	100.0	100.0	—	100.0
Psychologist (doctoral-level)	45.0	58.1	88.1	50.2
Psychologist (master's-level)	22.2	69.2	50.0	27.9
Social worker	22.0	68.2	30.1	28.1
Total	31.7	68.4	39.1	37.7
Total (active-duty and civilian providers) (%)	Army	Navy	Air Force	Total
Psychiatrist	76.7	73.7	92.6	79.2
Psychiatric nurse practitioner	100.0	100.0	100.0	100.0
Psychologist (doctoral-level)	42.8	52.1	73.9	50.1
Psychologist (master's-level)	21.1	66.7	23.4	25.8
Social worker	20.9	62.9	26.6	26.8
Total	34.5	64.5	48.0	42.7

pendently. Due to the small number of master's-level psychologists, we also did not attempt to power substrata defined by this provider type. Instead, we powered substrata that combined social workers with master's-level psychologists. In all, we designed sampling rates to power 12 total MHP substrata (defined by three service branches and four provider types, in which master's-level psychologists and social workers were combined into a single provider type). We aimed to have a minimum of 50 eligible respondents in each of these 12 substrata.

To determine the expected number of eligible respondents within a stratum, we estimated eligibility proportions and response rates for each substratum based on previous RAND research (Hepner et al., 2017). The expected number of eligible respondents was determined by the product of stratum size, sampling proportion, eligibility rate, and response rate. Where it was not possible to attain adequate power due to the population size of a stratum, the entire substratum was sampled. For example, all mental health nurse practitioners were sampled due to their small numbers.

Raw Response Rates and Eligibility

Tables A.5 and A.6 display the raw response rates by sampling strata. We note that these raw response rates are not equivalent to the American Association for Public Opinion Research response rates reported in Chapter Two. Stratum-level raw response rates reported in Tables A.5 and A.6 are simply the number of respondents divided by the size of the sampled stratum. For these tables, a respondent was defined as an individual who consented and completed any portion of the survey. This includes individuals who (1) consented and completed at least one question in the survey (550 BHTs and 665 MHPs) or (2) consented but were terminated from the survey based on their eligibility (15 BHTs and 105 MHPs). We used this as the operational definition of a respondent for the purposes of computing nonresponse weights.

TABLE A.5

BHT Raw Response Rates, by Service Branch

Active-Duty Service Members	Army	Navy	Air Force	Total
BHT (%)	38.0	45.0	47.4	43.1

TABLE A.6
MHP Raw Response Rates, by Stratum

Active-Duty Service Member (%)	Army	Navy	Air Force	Total
Psychiatrist	42.2	46.2	45.4	44.4
Psychiatric nurse practitioner	44.3	47.1	39.1	43.3
Psychologist (doctoral-level)	48.4	53.7	52.5	51.8
Psychologist (master's-level)	40.0	50.0	29.4	35.5
Social worker	54.5	26.2	39.7	41.3
Total	45.6	45.1	44.8	45.2
Civilian (%)	Army	Navy	Air Force	Total
Psychiatrist	29.0	29.7	0.0	27.8
Psychiatric nurse practitioner	50.0	42.9	0.0	45.0
Psychologist (doctoral-level)	37.1	38.9	37.8	37.5
Psychologist (master's-level)	34.9	27.8	0.0	32.3
Social worker	38.5	35.3	34.5	37.0
Total	36.4	35.4	33.3	35.7
Total (active-duty and civilian providers) (%)	Army	Navy	Air Force	Total
Psychiatrist	36.8	42.2	43.1	40.0
Psychiatric nurse practitioner	44.7	45.8	39.1	43.5
Psychologist (doctoral-level)	39.5	46.0	48.5	43.3
Psychologist (master's-level)	35.8	31.8	27.8	33.3
Social worker	41.3	32.9	36.7	38.1
Total	39.6	40.3	41.7	40.3

NOTES: Includes providers who were deemed ineligible; $n = 807$.

In interpreting these raw response rates, it is important to note that not all sampled MHPs were eligible to participate in the study. At the beginning of the survey, sampled MHPs were required to answer a single eligibility screening item to determine whether or not they had worked with a BHT in the past 12 months. While we were ultimately interested in characterizing the population of eligible MHPs, eligibility status was not known a priori. Importantly, we did not know the eligibility status of nonrespondents. We address the statistical implications of this limitation in our discussion of nonresponse weighting later in this appendix. For this reason, the raw response rates reported for MHPs do not necessarily reflect the response rates of eligible MHPs. If eligible providers had a higher probability of completing the screener than ineligible providers, then the raw response rates reported here would be lower than the true response rates among the population of eligible providers. By contrast, because all active BHTs were eligible for the survey, no eligibility screener was presented. However, 15 respondents from the BHT sample were determined to be ineligible during the interview and were therefore terminated from the survey.

Overall, approximately 43 percent of sampled BHTs and 41 percent of sampled MHPs responded to the survey, according to this definition. These raw response rates were typically higher for active-duty MHPs compared to civilian MHPs. Among those MHPs that did respond to the eligibility screener, approximately 87 percent were eligible (i.e., responded that they had worked with a BHT in the past 12 months). This figure varied by provider type, ranging from 82.3 percent for responding doctoral psychologists to 94.4 percent of responding psychiatrists. This also varied somewhat by service branch with eligibility rates of 84.8 percent, 85.3 percent, and 92.1 percent for the Army, Navy, and Air Force, respectively.

Analytic Sample

Tables A.7 and A.8 detail the final analytic sample of BHTs and MHPs, respectively. Our final analytic sample of BHTs consisted of 538 individuals out of the 1,311 sampled technicians (41.0 percent). Our final analytic cohort of MHPs consisted of 685 respondents out of the 1,984 sampled providers (34.5 percent). These rates are similar to that in a previous survey of MHPs (Hepner et al., 2017) in which 35.9 percent of sampled providers were ultimately included in the analytic sample. A small number of respondents were excluded from the analytic sample if it was determined (either from their responses to survey items or their responses to the screener) that they were ineligible for participation. Details regarding these exclusions are provided in Chapter Two.

TABLE A.7
BHT Analytic Cohort, by Service Branch

Active-Duty Service Members	Army	Navy	Air Force	Total
BHT	194	103	241	538

TABLE A.8
MHP Analytic Cohort, by Stratum

Active-Duty Service Members	Army	Navy	Air Force	Total
Psychiatrist	57	52	57	166
Psychiatric nurse practitioner	27	14	17	58
Psychologist (doctoral-level)	28	33	48	109
Psychologist (master's-level)	4	2	5	11
Social worker	27	11	25	63
Total	143	112	152	407
Civilians	Army	Navy	Air Force	Total
Psychiatrist	25	11	0	36
Psychiatric nurse practitioner	3	2	0	5
Psychologist (doctoral-level)	61	20	8	89
Psychologist (master's-level)	15	1	0	16
Social worker	80	28	24	132
Total	184	62	32	278
Total (active-duty and civilian providers)	Army	Navy	Air Force	Total
Psychiatrist	82	63	57	202
Psychiatric nurse practitioner	30	16	17	63
Psychologist (doctoral-level)	89	53	56	198
Psychologist (master's-level)	19	3	5	27
Social worker	107	39	49	195
Total	327	174	184	685

Weighting

Each individual respondent in our sample is assigned a weight w_i. Unless otherwise noted, all results on presented in this report incorporate weighting. For example, averages typically represent weighted averages $(\sum w_i Y_i)/(\sum w_i)$ rather than simple averages $(\sum Y_i)/n$. Weighting is performed so that reported results reflect the two target populations of interest: (1) all BHTs and (2) all MHPs working with BHTs. Unweighted summaries would not necessarily reflect these target populations.

The final weight w_i is equal to the product of a design weight w_i^D and a nonresponse weight w_i^N. The design weight accounts for the disproportionate sampling between individual strata. The nonresponse weight adjusts for differences between survey respondents and nonrespondents.

Design Weights

Design weights are incorporated to account for the disproportionate allocation in our sampling design. Disproportionate allocation was used to ensure that substrata of interest were sampled at high enough rates to provide statistical power for analyses of substrata. However, disproportionate allocation results in a final sample that is not representative of the target population. Design weights set equal to the inverse of the sampling probability correct for the nonrepresentativeness incurred by the sampling design. The sampling probabilities of the three BHT sampling strata and 30 MHP sampling strata are detailed in Tables A.3 and A.4, respectively. All individuals within the same stratum (e.g., all active-duty psychiatrists in the Army) receive the same design weight. We did not perform any trimming on the design weights, as extreme weights were not observed.

Nonresponse Weights

Nonresponse can bias analyses if nonrespondents differ from respondents on outcomes of interest. To account for this potential source of bias, nonresponse weights were computed for each respondent using propensity score methodology. The propensity score for an individual corresponds to the probability that individual responds to the survey, conditional on observed covariates. In particular, if R_i is a binary random variable that equals 1 for respondents and $\mathbf{X}_i$ is a set of observed covariates, then the propensity score of individual i is equal to $P(R_i=1|\mathbf{X}_i)$. For an outcome of interest Y_i, data are considered missing at random if $P(R_i=1|\mathbf{X}_i,Y_i)=P(R_i=1|\mathbf{X}_i)$. Intuitively, the missing at random assumption conveys the idea that observed covariates are capable of controlling for confounding between response and outcome. Standard statistical results show that, under this assumption, a nonresponse weight equal to the inverse of the propensity score corrects for nonresponse bias. The missing at random assumption is difficult to test in practice, as outcomes of nonrespondents are not measured and is more believable when $\mathbf{X}_i$ is a rich set of covariates. If an important variable is not included in the observed covariates $\mathbf{X}_i$ that is associated with both outcomes and response, then propensity score weighting is not guaranteed to remove all nonresponse bias.

In practice, the propensity scores must be estimated using statistical models fit to available data. The available covariate set $\mathbf{X}_i$ must therefore be observed for both respondents and nonrespondents. In this particular work, a limitation is the unknown eligibility status of nonresponding MHPs. While the nonresponse model would ideally only include individuals from the eligible population, eligibility of MHPs is only known for the respondents. However, if eligible and ineligible individuals had the same probability of responding, conditional on their observed covariates $\mathbf{X}_i$, then computed propensity scores based on the eligible and ineligible populations would reflect propensity scores based on just the eligible population, and no bias would be introduced. Another instance in which no bias would be introduced is if propensity scores in the combined (eligible and ineligible) population differed from the propensity scores in the eligible population by a fixed constant. If, however, eligibility affects the propensity scores of individuals differentially with different $\mathbf{X}_i$, then inaccuracies in propensity scores due to unknown eligibility may result in bias. Since eligibility is known only among respondents, such violations are not directly testable. These assumptions are consistent with those made in a prior survey analysis of MHPs (Hepner et al., 2017).

To estimate propensity scores in practice, we used the RAND-developed Toolkit for Weighting and Analysis of Nonequivalent Groups (TWANG), an R software package (Ridgeway et al., 2014). The TWANG method utilizes generalized boosted regression to estimate propensity scores. The advantages of generalized boosted regression over more traditional approaches (e.g., logistic regression) is that it is adaptive and non-parametric, iterating over many functional forms of all possible interactions. Model selection is governed by balance criteria between the populations of respondents and nonrespondents. A separate statistical model was fit for the BHT and MHP populations. For the BHTs, the variables that were included in the non-response model were service branch, gender, race, ethnicity, and paygrade. For the MHPs, the variables that were included in the nonresponse model were provider type, service branch, gender, duty status (active-duty versus civilian), race, and ethnicity.

For both BHT and MHP populations, propensity score weighting resulted in excellent balance in that nonrespondents and respondents had similar distributions on modeled covariates. We performed Kolmogorov-Smirnov tests for all modeled variables to test the null hypothesis that respondents and nonrespondents had the same distributions in the weighted populations. Before weighting, there were statistically significant discrepancies between respondents and nonrespondents with respect to service branch, race, and paygrade for BHTs and duty status and ethnicity for MHPs. After weighting, there were no statistically significant discrepancies between respondents and nonrespondents for either BHTs or MHPs. The smallest recorded Kolmogorov-Smirnov p-value was 0.54 for BHTs and 0.98 for MHPs. Smaller p-values indicate evidence against the null that respondents and nonrespondents are the same. We did not perform any trimming of nonresponse weights, as extreme weights were not observed.

Survey Development and Domains

In this appendix, we describe the development of our parallel surveys designed to assess BHT and MHP perspectives on BHT practice in the military. First, we describe the process we used to develop the surveys and obtain stakeholder input. Subsequently, we describe each survey domain, including the basis for the survey items, similarities and differences between the BHT and MHP versions of the survey, and the total number of items in each domain. The survey content can be found in Appendix C (BHT survey) and Appendix D (MHP survey).

Survey Development

In developing the survey, we drew from existing, validated scales to the extent possible. We conducted a targeted search to identify surveys that assessed the roles of care extenders (e.g., physician assistants), the roles of paraprofessionals in other settings (e.g., education), and training and supervision of mental health providers (e.g., psychology interns). We were interested in items that might be relevant to our surveys, such as those assessing the perceived quality of supervision and training. We also were interested in identifying the approaches that such surveys had taken in assessing care extender roles (e.g., by assessing frequency of specific tasks) or barriers to integrating these staff into clinical settings. To assess practice attributes and characteristics of the military experience (e.g., deployment history, satisfaction with military work), we drew from prior surveys of service members and military MHPs, including the 2018 Health Related Behaviors Survey (Meadows et al., 2021) and SOFS (U.S. Department of Defense, Office of People Analytics, 2017).

However, many of the domains of interest required items that were not available in existing, validated measures. For example, we were interested in the various roles that BHTs fill in clinical settings, as well as how the nature of these roles is shaped by the BHT training programs and specific policy documents from across service branches. In addition, although some barriers to integrating BHTs into clinical settings might be similar to those experienced by other types of care extenders in nonmilitary settings, some of the barriers that we identified in our curriculum, policy, and literature review (Holliday et al., 2019) were much more specific to the role of BHTs in the MHS (e.g., the possibility that active-duty MHPs might be more comfortable relying on BHTs than civilian providers would be) (Holliday et al., 2019). Therefore, we developed several items based on the findings in our previous report. However, even in developing those items, we drew on existing approaches to assessing job roles (e.g., response options for measuring frequency of specific tasks or proficiency with specific tasks).

After developing drafts of the BHT and MHP surveys, we put them through an iterative review and revision process. First, the surveys were reviewed by four RAND researchers with extensive experience with the MHS, surveying service members and military providers, or conducting job analyses. They were also reviewed by a RAND Army research fellow with experience as a practicing MHP in the MHS. In addition, we received input from the BHTWG. The Behavioral Health Clinical Community reviewed the revised survey content before it was finalized.

In the sections that follow, we describe the content of the BHT and MHP surveys, including the source of items that were adapted from existing measures and the rationales for those developed specifically for this survey. When we were able to include items from existing measures, it was generally only one to two items, so data on psychometric properties were not available and are not reported here. The two versions of the surveys were designed to be parallel for most items so that we could compare BHT and MHP perspectives on the topics assessed (i.e., BHT responsibilities, training and supervision, barriers to effective practice, changes to BHT practice, and satisfaction). The BHT survey contained 95 items, and the MHP survey consisted of 88 items.

Eligibility Screening

All active-duty BHTs were eligible to participate in the survey, so we did not include an eligibility screening item. Although our sampling information indicated that the sampled MHPs were either uniformed or DoD civilian providers, we did not know whether they had recent experience working with a BHT. Therefore, we included a single eligibility screening item to assess this. Specifically, MHPs were required to have worked with a uniformed BHT in the previous year.

Demographics, Service, and Practice Characteristics

The surveys asked BHTs and providers a series of questions to assess their sociodemographic characteristics, including race and ethnicity; military status (e.g., active component, National Guard/reserve, DoD civilian); and branch of service, using items adapted from Hepner et al. (2017). MHPs were also asked to indicate their professional discipline (i.e., clinical psychologist, licensed clinical social worker; master's-level, licensed professional counselor; psychiatrist; or psychiatric nurse practitioner). These variables were also available in the data from DMDC's Health Manpower Personnel Data System. For race/ethnicity and professional discipline, we used DMDC data if a survey response was not available. For military status and branch of service, we used DMDC data in our analyses rather than the survey responses.

For both BHTs and MHPs, we assessed years in practice using an item adapted from a previous survey of MHPs (Hepner et al., 2017). We also assessed the current settings in which BHTs and providers interact with patients, with response options guided by our review of the literature and discussions with key stakeholders (Holliday et al., 2019). We asked BHTs to indicate the nature of their current assignment (in garrison versus deployed, medical versus operational), given our previous findings suggesting that scope of work is influenced by unit type and setting (Holliday et al., 2019). Both BHTs and MHPs were also asked whether they had deployed in the previous 12 months using an item adapted from the DoD Health Related Behaviors Survey (Meadows et al., 2021). MHPs were additionally asked whether they had worked with a BHT while deployed. Finally, providers were asked to indicate how long they had practiced as a mental health clinician in the MHS.

The BHT survey included eight items on demographics, service, and practice characteristics, and the MHP survey included ten.

BHT Responsibilities

We developed a series of questions to learn more about BHTs' typical responsibilities. BHTs began by estimating the percentage of duty hours in a typical week (totaling 100 percent) spent on each of four categories of tasks: responsibilities related to patient care, administrative clinical responsibilities, nonclinical responsibilities, and other responsibilities. When indicating other responsibilities, BHTs were asked to specify the type of activities. Response options were informed by the first phase of this project (Holliday et al., 2019). MHPs were asked an initial question about whether they had a leadership position at their clinic.

We developed a list of 22 tasks that might fall within a BHT's scope of clinical responsibilities, based on our review of the literature and policy-related documents across the services (Holliday et al., 2019). We grouped tasks into four categories: screening and assessment, psychosocial interventions, case management, and outreach and resilience activities. BHTs were asked to indicate how frequently they performed each task, with response options on a five-point scale ranging from "never" to "very often." They also reported how proficient they believed themselves to be in performing each task, with responses on a four-point scale ranging from "I cannot perform this task" to "I can perform this task with no assistance and I can train someone to perform this task" (response options from Lytell et al., 2017, and Pynes, 2009). MHPs were asked to indicate how frequently the BHTs they worked with performed each task, as well as their perception of BHTs' proficiency in completing each task (response options adapted from Lytell et al., 2017, and Pynes, 2009).

BHTs who indicated that they had deployed in the previous 12 months were asked an additional set of questions about their responsibilities while deployed. These BHTs were first asked whether they had most recently deployed with a medical or operational unit, given some evidence to suggest that responsibilities differ by unit type (Holliday et al., 2019). They were then asked to indicate whether, while deployed, they had performed each task more often, less often, or a similar amount than when they were assigned to an MTF in garrison. Participants could indicate that they had not been assigned to an MTF in garrison in the past; Army and Navy BHTs are eligible to deploy immediately after completing training (Holliday et al., 2019). These questions were asked with respect to the four higher-level task categories (i.e., screening and assessment, psychosocial interventions, case management, and outreach and resilience).

Both BHTs and MHPs were asked to indicate whether BHTs performed tasks that were outside their scope of practice. Respondents were able to indicate in which settings this occurred (i.e., deployed settings, in garrison, or both) and were asked to describe the tasks.

The BHT survey included 55 items on BHT responsibilities, and the MHP survey included 46 items.

Training and Supervision

Both BHTs and MHPs were asked a series of questions about the perceived adequacy of the training that BHTs receive, including classroom instruction at METC, clinical practicum experience at METC, on the job training, and continuing training. Response options included "spent too much time," "spent about the right amount of time," or "spent too little time." Both groups were also asked to indicate whether they believe BHTs receive adequate supervision to perform their clinical duties using an item adapted from a study of paraprofessional perceptions of training and professional development (Stratton, 2014), with responses including yes, no, or unsure.

In addition, BHTs were asked to indicate which types of mental health providers they support in their current clinical setting, with options including doctoral-level clinical psychologists, social workers, master's-level psychologists, psychiatrists or psychiatric nurse practitioners, or other. Providers were asked if they provide clinical supervision to a BHT with an item adapted from Stratton (2014) (yes/no).

The BHT survey and MHP surveys each included seven items in this domain.

Barriers to Effective BHT Practice

We included a series of questions to determine what barriers BHTs and MHPs perceived to integrating BHTs into clinical settings. Drawing on our earlier research (Holliday et al., 2019), we developed 11 statements to represent potential barriers identified in the literature and through key stakeholder discussions (e.g., "Licensed mental health providers have limited time to invest in ongoing supervision and training of behavioral health technicians"). Respondents were asked to indicate the extent to which they agreed with each statement on a five-point scale ranging from "strongly disagree" to "strongly agree."

The BHT and MHP surveys each included 11 items on barriers to BHT practice.

Satisfaction

Both BHTs and MHPs were asked to rate their satisfaction with their current military job using two items from the SOFS (U.S. Department of Defense, Office of People Analytics, 2017): satisfaction with the type of work they do in their military job and the quality of their supervisor. We selected these items because they allowed for comparison with the overall active-duty population. Responses were made on a five-point scale ranging from "very dissatisfied" to "very satisfied." BHTs were also asked two questions to assess their perceived fit with the BHT job, including whether their personality was a good match for the job and whether they were the right person for this type of work (Lauver and Kristof-Brown, 2001). Response options for these two items were on a seven-point scale ranging from "strongly disagree" to "strongly agree." We also asked MHPs to indicate their level of satisfaction with BHTs' performance, with responses on a five-point scale ranging from "very dissatisfied" to "very satisfied."

The BHT survey included four items in this domain, and the MHP survey included two items.

Perceptions of Potential Changes to BHT Practice

We assessed BHT and MHP perspectives on potential changes to BHT practice. Specifically, through the literature review and stakeholder discussions we conducted in the first phase of this project, we identified a number of recommendations for using BHTs more effectively as care extenders in the MHS. We developed ten items to reflect these potential practice changes. Respondents were asked to indicate the extent to which they believed each option would enable BHTs to be more effective—for example, "Provide templates, checklists, or forms to structure clinical tasks (e.g., clinical interviews) for behavioral health technicians" and "Provide education to licensed mental health providers on how they can utilize behavioral health technicians." Responses were made on a five-point scale and ranged from "not at all" to "extremely."

The BHT survey included ten items in this domain, and the MHP survey included 11 items.

Comparing the BHT and MHP Surveys

Table B.1 summarizes the content of the BHT and MHP surveys, including the broader domains described in this appendix; topics assessed; item source, including whether it was taken or adapted from a previous survey or developed specifically for this survey; and the number of items used to assess each topic on each survey. Table B.2 shows BHT- and MHP-reported frequency and proficiency items used to compute the subscores reported in Chapter Four.

TABLE B.1

BHT and MHP Survey Content and Sources

Domain and Topics Assessed	Items	Source	Number of Items BHT Survey	MHP Survey
Eligibility screen				
Worked with BHT in past year	Eligibility	RAND	N/A	1
Demographics, service, and practice characteristics				
Demographics and service characteristics	Gender	DMDC	N/A	N/A
	Rank	DMDC	N/A	N/A
	Age	DMDC	N/A	N/A
	Race/ethnicity	Hepner et al., 2017	2	2
	Military status	Hepner et al., 2017	1	1
	Branch of service	Hepner et al., 2017	1	1
	Provider type	Hepner et al., 2017	0	1
Practice attributes	Years in practice	Hepner et al., 2017	1	1
	Current assignment	RAND	1	0
	Years in MHS	RAND	0	1
	Leadership position in clinic	RAND	0	1
	Provides supervision to BHTs	Adapted from Stratton, 2014	0	1
	Type of providers supported	RAND	1	0
	Current treatment setting	RAND	1	1
BHT responsibilities				
BHT time spent on tasks	Percentage of time spent on administrative, clinical, and nonclinical responsibilities	RAND	4	0
Clinical responsibilities	Activities rated on frequency/proficiency	RAND/Pynes, 2009; Lytell et al., 2017	44	44

Table B.1—Continued

Domain and Topics Assessed	Items	Source	Number of Items	
			BHT Survey	MHP Survey
Clinical responsibilities during deployment	Deployed in past 12 months	Adapted from DoD Health Related Behaviors Survey	1	1
	Deployed with BHTs	RAND	0	1
	Type of deployment	RAND	2	0
	Frequency of clinical activities during deployment	RAND	4	0
Training and supervision				
Adequacy of training	Adequacy of METC instruction	RAND	1	1
	METC practicum	RAND	1	1
	OJT	RAND	1	1
	Continuing education	RAND	1	1
Adequacy of supervision	Adequate supervision of clinical activities	Adapted from Stratton, 2014	1	1
Responsibilities outside of scope	BHTs asked to perform responsibilities out of scope and setting	RAND	2	2
Barriers to effective BHT practice				
Barriers	Perceptions of 11 barriers	RAND/Hepner et al., 2017	11	11
Satisfaction				
Satisfaction	Satisfaction with type of work and quality of supervisor	RAND/SOFS	2	2
BHT fit for the job	Personality matches job	Lauver and Kristof-Brown, 2001	1	0
	Right type of person for this work	Lauver and Kristof-Brown, 2001	1	0

Table B.1—Continued

Domain and Topics Assessed	Items	Source	Number of Items BHT Survey	MHP Survey
Perceptions of potential changes to BHT practice				
Provider perceptions of BHT performance	Satisfaction with BHT work	RAND	0	1
Potential changes	Perceptions of 10 potential changes	RAND	10	10
Total items			95	88

TABLE B.2
BHT Task Subscores and Specific Tasks Within Each Subscore

Subscore	Task
Screening/assessment	Triage walk-in patients
	Administer/score symptom measures
	Intake interviews
	Use Behavioral Health Data Portal
	Administer/score psychological tests
	Administer/score neuropsychological tests
	Risk assessments
Psychosocial interventions	Supportive counseling for mental health concerns
	Supportive counseling for substance use
	Psychotherapy for mental health
	Psychotherapy for substance use disorders
	Group counseling sessions
	Psychoeducational groups
Treatment planning/monitoring	Develop treatment plans
	Review patient homework
	Case management
	Monitor patient progress using symptom measures
	Assess medication adherence/side effects
Outreach/planning	Conduct behavioral health outreach
	Combat stress interventions
	Conduct prevention outreach
	Consult in non–behavioral health clinical settings

BHT Survey

Informed Consent

[*TELEPHONE*] Before we begin, I need to read through some important and relevant information regarding this study. Though we already briefly touched on some of these details, the information that I'll review will make sure you have a complete understanding of this study and its purpose.

[*WEB TITLE*] Optimizing the Role of Military Behavioral Health Technicians

[*TELEPHONE INTRO*] You have been invited to participate in a survey about your role as a uniformed behavioral health technician. Behavioral health technicians are also referred to as psych techs or L24A in the Navy; behavioral health specialists or Sixty-Eight X-Rays in the Army; or mental health technicians, or Four Charlies in the Air Force. For the remainder of the survey, we use the term "behavioral health technician" to describe your occupation. Through this survey, we aim to learn about your training and supervision, along with ways that the roles of behavioral health technicians could be expanded or changed.

[*WEB INTRO*] You have been invited to participate in a survey about your role as a uniformed behavioral health technician (L24A), behavioral health specialist (68X), or mental health technician (4C0X1). For the remainder of the survey, we use the term "behavioral health technician" to describe your occupation. Through this survey, we aim to learn about your training and supervision, along with ways that the roles of behavioral health technicians could be expanded or changed.

[*TELEPHONE AND WEB*] The RAND Corporation, a private, nonprofit research institution, is conducting this research project, which is funded by the Department of Defense (DoD) through the Psychological Health Center of Excellence. Davis Research is working with RAND to conduct the survey.

The survey will take approximately 30 minutes to complete online, or 40 minutes if you complete it by telephone. While there is no direct benefit to you for participation in this research project, our findings could help to optimize the use of behavioral health technicians within the Military Health System (MHS). If you complete the survey during off-duty time, we will provide a $50 Amazon gift card as a token of appreciation. You may complete the survey during duty time, if you decline the gift card incentive.

Your participation in this survey is entirely voluntary. If you do decide to participate, you can skip questions or stop taking the survey at any time. Choosing not to participate or not to answer some questions will not result in any penalty.

Disclosure of survey responses could cause personal or professional embarrassment. However, the risk of disclosure is minimal due to the difficulty in identifying individuals and the care that will be taken by the personnel who have access to the data. We will protect the confidentiality of your responses, and your supervisor will not have access to the information you provide. [*NEXT SENTENCE WEB ONLY*] Information you provide will not be linked to your email address or IP address. RAND will not include any participant names in any reports. The RAND Corporation's Human Subjects Protection Committee and the Defense Health Agency Headquarters Human Research Protection Program have reviewed and approved the study procedures. Representatives of DoD are authorized to review our research records.

The DoD Privacy Advisory states that the Defense Manpower Data Center has provided certain information about you to allow RAND to conduct this survey. Your name and contact information have been used to send you notifications and information about this survey. The Defense Manpower Data Center has provided certain demographic information to reduce the number of questions in the survey and minimize the burden on your time. Using a unique participant ID, your responses will be linked with these demographic data by RAND to allow for a thorough analysis of the responses by demographics. RAND has not been authorized by DoD to identify or link survey responses and demographic information with your name and contact information. The resulting reports will only include analysis of respondent groupings of 5 or more so that no individual could be identified.

We would be happy to answer any questions you might have about the study or your participation. For more information about this survey, you may contact:

Kimberly Hepner, Ph.D.
Senior Behavioral Scientist, RAND Corporation
Tel: (310) 393-0411 ext. 6381
Email: Kimberly_Hepner@rand.org

If you have questions about your rights as a research participant or need to report a research-related injury or concern, you can contact RAND's Human Subjects Protection Committee toll-free at (866) 697-5620 or by emailing hspcinfo@rand.org. If possible, when you contact the Committee, please reference Study #2018-0138.

This survey received all required human subjects and regulatory approvals. The survey Report Control Symbol (RCS) license number is DD-HA-2703 (Washington Headquarters Services).

[*WEB*] Please indicate whether you consent to participate in this study.
[*TELEPHONE*] Do you consent to participate in this study?

__ Yes, I agree to participate.
__ I do not want to participate in this study and I would like to exit the survey now.

[*WEB*] As you take the survey, please do not include any personally identifiable information in your responses. Any identifiable information inadvertently provided within the survey will be removed from the data and reporting of results.

[*TELEPHONE*] Please do not include any personally identifiable information with your responses. Any identifiable information inadvertently provided within the survey will be removed from the data and reporting of results.

Survey Items

Practice Attributes

[*For all items, allow respondents to skip past them without answering the question. Unless otherwise specified in the coding instructions, skip to the next item. Display a message confirming that they intended to leave the question blank before continuing to next screen.*]

The first set of questions asks about your clinical experience and the settings in which you practice.

[*PROGRAMMING NOTE: Allow to enter year and not month; Display error message if months entered without years; Force years to 0 if >11 months entered.*]

PA1. How long have you been working as a behavioral health technician (beginning with your first placement after METC)?[a] [*TELEPHONE: You can give your answer in years and months.*]	____ years ____ months
PA2. Which of the following best describes your current assignment?	__ In garrison military treatment facility __ In garrison operational unit __ Deployed with a medical unit __ Deployed with an operational unit __ Other (please specify): _____
[a] Question adapted from Hepner et al., 2017.	

[PROGRAMMING NOTE: If PA2 = "Deployed with a medical unit" or "Deployed with an operational unit," skip PA4 (which should be backfilled as "Yes").]

PA3. Within the last month, in which settings have you spent time interacting with patients during duty hours? *[WEB: Please select all settings in which you currently work.]* *[TELEPHONE: I will quickly read a short list of possible options. Please let me know which ones apply to you in the last month.]*	__ Outpatient mental health (including intensive outpatient programs) __ Inpatient mental health __ Outpatient substance use __ Inpatient substance use __ Primary care __ Behavioral health (integrated mental health and substance use) __ Emergency department __ Other (please specify): _____ __ None __ Prefer not to answer
PA4. In the past 12 months, did you spend any time deployed, including both combat and non-combat zone deployments (excluding training missions)?[a]	__ Yes __ No

[a] Question adapted from DoD Health Related Behaviors Survey (see Meadows et al., 2021).

The next section asks about your role as a behavioral health technician, including both clinical and nonclinical responsibilities.

| RS1. [WEB] | The activities are: |
| What percentage of duty hours in a typical week do you spend on each of the following types of activities? (Should add up to 100%) [TELEPHONE: These numbers should add up to 100%.] [TELEPHONE, IF RESPONSES DO NOT ADD UP TO 100%: Those do not quite add up to 100%. Let me quickly review these again with you. The activities are . . . (repeat response options).] | __ Patient care–related clinical responsibilities (e.g., leading groups, conducting clinical interviews, performing prevention activities) __ Administrative clinic responsibilities (e.g., answering phones, making appointments) __ Nonclinical responsibilities (e.g., unit requirements, physical training) __ Other (please specify): _____ |

For the next set of questions, we are interested in the set of duties and tasks that you perform as part of your role as a behavioral health technician. For each of the following tasks, we will ask you how often you perform the task and how confident you are in performing the task.[1]

[WEB] For each item, please answer the following questions:

[TELEPHONE] For each item, you will be asked to answer the following two questions:

- How often do you currently perform each of the following tasks?
- How confident are you in performing each task?

[WEB NOTE: Each item-specific screen should begin with the item as noted below, and have the following two questions:]

- How often do you currently perform this task?
- How confident are you in performing this task?

---

[1] In this set of questions, response options drew on Pynes, 2009, and Lytell et al., 2017.

[*TELEPHONE: For each item, read the item, then ask:*

- *(ITEM_F) Do you perform this task . . . (read options)?*
- *(ITEM_C) Which of the following best describes how confident are you are in performing this task?*]

[*TELEPHONE NOTE: Please read the text in parentheses for each question. "i.e." should be read as "that is"; "e.g." should be read as "for example."*]

The first set of questions will ask about screening and assessment.

RS2. [*TELEPHONE: The first task is*] Triage walk-in patients (i.e., briefly assess patient need and determine need for care)	RS2_F. Frequency: __ Never __ Rarely __ Sometimes __ Often __ Very often	RS2_C. Confidence: __ I cannot perform this task. __ I can perform this task with assistance. __ I can perform this task with no assistance. __ I can perform this task with no assistance and I can train someone to perform this task.
RS3. Use the Behavioral Health Data Portal (BHDP)	RS3_F. Frequency: __ Never __ Rarely __ Sometimes __ Often __ Very often	RS3_C. Confidence: __ I cannot perform this task. __ I can perform this task with assistance. __ I can perform this task with no assistance. __ I can perform this task with no assistance and I can train someone to perform this task.

RS4. Administer and score behavioral health symptom measures (e.g., PHQ-9, PCL, AUDIT-C)	RS4_F. Frequency: __ Never __ Rarely __ Sometimes __ Often __ Very often	RS4_C. Confidence: __ I cannot perform this task. __ I can perform this task with assistance. __ I can perform this task with no assistance. __ I can perform this task with no assistance and I can train someone to perform this task.
RS5. Perform intake interviews/ evaluations (e.g., history of current problem)	RS5_F. Frequency: __ Never __ Rarely __ Sometimes __ Often __ Very often	RS5_C. Confidence: __ I cannot perform this task. __ I can perform this task with assistance. __ I can perform this task with no assistance. __ I can perform this task with no assistance and I can train someone to perform this task.
RS6. Administer and score psychological tests (e.g., MMPI)	RS6_F. Frequency: __ Never __ Rarely __ Sometimes __ Often __ Very often	RS6_C. Confidence: __ I cannot perform this task. __ I can perform this task with assistance. __ I can perform this task with no assistance. __ I can perform this task with no assistance and I can train someone to perform this task.

RS7. Administer and score cognitive and neuropsychological tests (e.g., RBANS, WAIS)	RS7_F. Frequency: __ Never __ Rarely __ Sometimes __ Often __ Very often	RS7_C. Confidence: __ I cannot perform this task. __ I can perform this task with assistance. __ I can perform this task with no assistance. __ I can perform this task with no assistance and I can train someone to perform this task.
RS8. Perform risk assessments (e.g., suicide risk, homicide risk)	RS8_F. Frequency: __ Never __ Rarely __ Sometimes __ Often __ Very often	RS8_C. Confidence: __ I cannot perform this task. __ I can perform this task with assistance. __ I can perform this task with no assistance. __ I can perform this task with no assistance and I can train someone to perform this task.

The next set of questions will ask about psychosocial interventions.

RS9. [TELEPHONE: The first task is] Provide supportive counseling for mental health concerns	RS9_F. Frequency: __ Never __ Rarely __ Sometimes __ Often __ Very often	RS9_C. Confidence: __ I cannot perform this task. __ I can perform this task with assistance. __ I can perform this task with no assistance. __ I can perform this task with no assistance and I can train someone to perform this task.

RS10. Provide supportive counseling for substance use disorders or alcohol or drug use concerns	RS10_F. Frequency: __ Never __ Rarely __ Sometimes __ Often __ Very often	RS10_C. Confidence: __ I cannot perform this task. __ I can perform this task with assistance. __ I can perform this task with no assistance. __ I can perform this task with no assistance and I can train someone to perform this task.
RS11. Deliver specific evidence-based psychotherapy for mental health concerns (e.g., cognitive behavioral therapy for depression)	RS11_F. Frequency: __ Never __ Rarely __ Sometimes __ Often __ Very often	RS11_C. Confidence: __ I cannot perform this task. __ I can perform this task with assistance. __ I can perform this task with no assistance. __ I can perform this task with no assistance and I can train someone to perform this task.
RS12. Deliver specific evidence-based psychotherapy for substance use disorders (e.g., cognitive behavioral relapse prevention therapy)	RS12_F. Frequency: __ Never __ Rarely __ Sometimes __ Often __ Very often	RS12_C. Confidence: __ I cannot perform this task. __ I can perform this task with assistance. __ I can perform this task with no assistance. __ I can perform this task with no assistance and I can train someone to perform this task.

RS13. Facilitate group counseling or group therapy sessions	RS13_F. Frequency: __ Never __ Rarely __ Sometimes __ Often __ Very often	RS13_C. Confidence: __ I cannot perform this task. __ I can perform this task with assistance. __ I can perform this task with no assistance. __ I can perform this task with no assistance and I can train someone to perform this task.
RS14. Facilitate psychoeducational groups (e.g., stress management, smoking cessation)	RS14_F. Frequency: __ Never __ Rarely __ Sometimes __ Often __ Very often	RS14_C. Confidence: __ I cannot perform this task. __ I can perform this task with assistance. __ I can perform this task with no assistance. __ I can perform this task with no assistance and I can train someone to perform this task.

The next set of questions will ask about case management.

RS15. [TELEPHONE: The first task is] Develop treatment plans	RS15_F. Frequency: __ Never __ Rarely __ Sometimes __ Often __ Very often	RS15_C. Confidence: __ I cannot perform this task. __ I can perform this task with assistance. __ I can perform this task with no assistance. __ I can perform this task with no assistance and I can train someone to perform this task.

RS16. Review patient homework (e.g., between session activities) or logs	RS16_F. Frequency: __ Never __ Rarely __ Sometimes __ Often __ Very often	RS16_C. Confidence: __ I cannot perform this task. __ I can perform this task with assistance. __ I can perform this task with no assistance. __ I can perform this task with no assistance and I can train someone to perform this task.
RS17. Perform case management activities (e.g., care coordination, referrals)	RS17_F. Frequency: __ Never __ Rarely __ Sometimes __ Often __ Very often	RS17_C. Confidence: __ I cannot perform this task. __ I can perform this task with assistance. __ I can perform this task with no assistance. __ I can perform this task with no assistance and I can train someone to perform this task.
RS18. Monitor patient progress during treatment over time using symptom measures (e.g., PHQ-9, PCL, GAD-7)	RS18_F. Frequency: __ Never __ Rarely __ Sometimes __ Often __ Very often	RS18_C. Confidence: __ I cannot perform this task. __ I can perform this task with assistance. __ I can perform this task with no assistance. __ I can perform this task with no assistance and I can train someone to perform this task.

RS19. Assess medication adherence and side effects	RS19_F. Frequency: __ Never __ Rarely __ Sometimes __ Often __ Very often	RS19_C. Confidence: __ I cannot perform this task. __ I can perform this task with assistance. __ I can perform this task with no assistance. __ I can perform this task with no assistance and I can train someone to perform this task.

The next set of questions will ask about outreach and resilience activities.

RS20. [*TELEPHONE: The first task is*] Conduct behavioral health outreach to units or base community to provide information about behavioral health services	RS20_F. Frequency: __ Never __ Rarely __ Sometimes __ Often __ Very often	RS20_C. Confidence: __ I cannot perform this task. __ I can perform this task with assistance. __ I can perform this task with no assistance. __ I can perform this task with no assistance and I can train someone to perform this task.
RS21. Conduct combat stress briefings, trainings, or interventions (e.g., Combat Operational Stress Control [COSC])	RS21_F. Frequency: __ Never __ Rarely __ Sometimes __ Often __ Very often	RS21_C. Confidence: __ I cannot perform this task. __ I can perform this task with assistance. __ I can perform this task with no assistance. __ I can perform this task with no assistance and I can train someone to perform this task.

RS22. Conduct community prevention, intervention, or outreach briefings to units or base community	RS22_F. Frequency: __ Never __ Rarely __ Sometimes __ Often __ Very often	RS22_C. Confidence: __ I cannot perform this task. __ I can perform this task with assistance. __ I can perform this task with no assistance. __ I can perform this task with no assistance and I can train someone to perform this task.
RS23. Provide behavioral health consultation in non-behavioral health clinical settings (e.g., in a medical or surgical setting)	RS23_F. Frequency: __ Never __ Rarely __ Sometimes __ Often __ Very often	RS23_C. Confidence: __ I cannot perform this task. __ I can perform this task with assistance. __ I can perform this task with no assistance. __ I can perform this task with no assistance and I can train someone to perform this task.

[PROGRAMMING NOTE: The next set of questions will be asked only of individuals who indicated that they deployed in the past 12 months. If PA4 = "yes," ask RS24–RS28. If PA4 = "no," skip to RS29.]

You indicated before that you deployed in the past twelve months. The next set of questions ask about your experiences while deployed.

RS24. During your most recent deployment, including any current deployment, were you assigned to a medical unit (e.g., combat support hospital, combat and operational stress control unit, area support medical company) or an operational unit (e.g., brigade combat team, division surgeon section, corps headquarters)?	__ Medical unit __ Operational unit

[PROGRAMMING NOTE: Ask RS24a only if RS24 is left blank.]

[TELEPHONE NOTE: Ask RS24a only if respondent notes that their deployment was not medical or operational.]

RS24a. Please describe the type of unit that you deployed with if it was something other than medical or operational.	(Free response box)

[WEB] During your most recent deployment, compared to times that you were assigned to an MTF in garrison, how often did you perform each of the following tasks?

[TELEPHONE] When answering the following items, please think about your most recent deployment. For each item, we will be asking how often you performed each task compared to times that you were assigned to an MTF in garrison.

[TELEPHONE NOTE: For each item, ask "Compared to times that you were assigned to an MTF in garrison, how often did you conduct (item)?"]

RS25. Screening and assessment (e.g., triage, intake interviews, administer and score tests)	___ Performed less often while deployed ___ Performed the same amount while deployed ___ Performed more often while deployed ___ I have not been assigned to an MTF in garrison in the past [PROGRAMMING NOTE: If RS25 = "I have not been assigned to an MTF in garrison in the past," skip to RS29.]
RS26. Psychosocial interventions (e.g., individual therapy, group therapy, psychoeducational groups)	___ Performed less often while deployed ___ Performed the same amount while deployed ___ Performed more often while deployed
RS27. Case management (e.g., develop treatment plans, care coordination, assess medication adherence)	___ Performed less often while deployed ___ Performed the same amount while deployed ___ Performed more often while deployed
RS28. Outreach and resilience tasks (e.g., combat stress interventions, outreach briefings to units)	___ Performed less often while deployed ___ Performed the same amount while deployed ___ Performed more often while deployed

[PROGRAMMING NOTE: The next question will be asked of all respondents.]

| RS29. Have you ever been asked to perform a task that exceeded your training or that you perceived to be outside your scope of practice as a behavioral health technician? [*TELEPHONE, IF YES: Was that only in deployed settings, only in garrison, or in both settings?*] | __ Yes, only in deployed settings
 __ Yes, only in garrison
 __ Yes, in deployed settings and in garrison
 __ No |

[*PROGRAMMING NOTE: If any yes response above, ask RS29a. If no, skip to SCT1.*]

| RS29a. Please describe these tasks in as much detail as possible. ***Do not enter personally identifiable information.*** | (Free response box) |

Supervision/Collaboration/Training

The next set of questions assesses your perceptions of your training and supervision.

[*WEB*] Please rate your perceptions about the time you have spent in each of the following training activities:

[*TELEPHONE*] Please answer each item with "spent too much time," "spent too little time," or "spent about the right amount of time."

| SCT1. Classroom instruction at METC | __ Spent too much time
 __ Spent too little time
 __ Spent about the right amount of time |

SCT2. Clinical practicum experience at METC	__ Spent too much time __ Spent too little time __ Spent about the right amount of time
SCT3. On-the-job training	__ Spent too much time __ Spent too little time __ Spent about the right amount of time
SCT4. Continuing education	__ Spent too much time __ Spent too little time __ Spent about the right amount of time

SCT5. What types of mental health providers do you support in your clinical setting? [WEB: Check all that apply.] [TELEPHONE: Please tell me all that apply.]	__ Clinical psychologist (Ph.D. or Psy.D.) __ Licensed clinical social worker (LCSW or MCSW) __ Master's-level, licensed professional counselor (e.g., LPC or LMHC) __ Psychiatrist (M.D. or D.O.) __ Psychiatric nurse practitioner __ Other (please specify): _____

SCT6. At this time, do you feel like you receive adequate supervision to perform your clinical duties as a behavioral health technician?[a]	__ Yes __ No __ Unsure

[a] Question adapted from Stratton, 2014.

Perceptions of and Barriers to Effective BHT Practice

The next questions assess your perceptions of behavioral health technicians and their roles within the Military Health System.

[*WEB*] Please indicate your level of agreement with the following statements:

[*TELEPHONE*] Please tell me to what extent you agree with each of the following statements. For each statement, please answer "strongly disagree," "disagree," "neither disagree nor agree," "agree," or "strongly agree."

[*TELEPHONE NOTE: Read response options for the first 2–3 items and then as needed.*]

PB1. Licensed mental health providers are not familiar with the range of clinical activities behavioral health technicians are trained to provide.	__ Strongly disagree __ Disagree __ Neither disagree nor agree __ Agree __ Strongly agree
PB2. [*TELEPHONE: The next one is*] Licensed mental health providers who were trained more recently are less comfortable relying on behavioral health technicians.	__ Strongly disagree __ Disagree __ Neither disagree nor agree __ Agree __ Strongly agree
PB3. [TELEPHONE: *The next one is*] Civilian licensed mental health providers are less familiar than uniformed licensed mental health providers with the clinical tasks that behavioral health technicians are trained to perform.	__ Strongly disagree __ Disagree __ Neither disagree nor agree __ Agree __ Strongly agree

PB4. [*TELEPHONE: The next one is*] Licensed mental health providers have limited time to invest in ongoing supervision and training of behavioral health technicians.	__ Strongly disagree __ Disagree __ Neither disagree nor agree __ Agree __ Strongly agree
PB5. [*TELEPHONE: The next one is*] Behavioral health technicians need more systematic supervision to effectively provide clinical care.	__ Strongly disagree __ Disagree __ Neither disagree nor agree __ Agree __ Strongly agree
PB6. [*TELEPHONE: The next one is*] Licensed mental health providers would be more comfortable sharing clinical tasks with behavioral health technicians if they had a credential (e.g., Certified Alcohol and Drug Counselor [CADC]).	__ Strongly disagree __ Disagree __ Neither disagree nor agree __ Agree __ Strongly agree
PB7. [*TELEPHONE: The next one is*] Behavioral health technicians are primarily needed to cover the administrative responsibilities in clinics.	__ Strongly disagree __ Disagree __ Neither disagree nor agree __ Agree __ Strongly agree
PB8. [*TELEPHONE: The next one is*] Behavioral health technicians have limited dedicated time spent in clinical settings due to other unit responsibilities.	__ Strongly disagree __ Disagree __ Neither disagree nor agree __ Agree __ Strongly agree

PB9. [*TELEPHONE: The next one is*] If licensed mental health providers integrate behavioral health technicians more into clinical care, they won't get "credit" for delivering the care (i.e., it won't help their RVUs).	__ Strongly disagree __ Disagree __ Neither disagree nor agree __ Agree __ Strongly agree
PB10. [*TELEPHONE: The next one is*] There can be substantial variability in behavioral health technician skills, even within the same rank.	__ Strongly disagree __ Disagree __ Neither disagree nor agree __ Agree __ Strongly agree
PB11. [*TELEPHONE: The next one is*] Behavioral health technicians would feel more comfortable receiving on-the-job training from a senior enlisted behavioral health technician than from a licensed mental health provider.	__ Strongly disagree __ Disagree __ Neither disagree nor agree __ Agree __ Strongly agree

The next set of statements describe potential changes for behavioral health technicians or the licensed mental health providers who work with them.

[*WEB*] Please indicate the extent to which each option would enable behavioral health technicians to be more effective within the Military Health System.

[*TELEPHONE*] To what extent would each of the following options enable behavioral health technicians to be more effective within the Military Health System? For each item, please answer "not at all," "slightly," "moderately," "very much," or "extremely."

[*TELEPHONE NOTE: Read response options for the first 2–3 items and then as needed.*]

PB13. Establish specific training plans for behavioral health technicians upon leaving the METC ("the Schoolhouse")	__ Not at all __ Slightly __ Moderately __ Very much __ Extremely
PB14. [*TELEPHONE: The next one is*] Provide templates, checklists, or forms to structure clinical tasks (e.g., clinical interviews) for behavioral health technicians	__ Not at all __ Slightly __ Moderately __ Very much __ Extremely
PB15. [*TELEPHONE: The next one is*] Provide education to licensed mental health providers on how they can utilize behavioral health technicians	__ Not at all __ Slightly __ Moderately __ Very much __ Extremely
PB16. [*TELEPHONE: The next one is*] Establish administrative policies to better define components of behavioral health technician work (e.g., expectations for roles, supervision)	__ Not at all __ Slightly __ Moderately __ Very much __ Extremely
PB17. [*TELEPHONE: The next one is*] Train behavioral health technicians to implement treatment approaches that are effective across multiple psychiatric diagnoses (e.g., problem solving therapy)	__ Not at all __ Slightly __ Moderately __ Very much __ Extremely

PB18. [*TELEPHONE: The next one is*] Train behavioral health technicians to implement evidence-based psychotherapies for lower risk patients (e.g., cognitive behavioral therapy for depression)	__ Not at all __ Slightly __ Moderately __ Very much __ Extremely
PB19. [*TELEPHONE: The next one is*] Train behavioral health technicians to implement evidence-based psychotherapies for more complex patients (e.g., cognitive processing therapy for PTSD)	__ Not at all __ Slightly __ Moderately __ Very much __ Extremely
PB20. [*TELEPHONE: The next one is*] Provide behavioral health technicians with opportunities to participate in ongoing professional development (e.g., courses through Army Medical Department Center and School, obtaining civilian credentials)	__ Not at all __ Slightly __ Moderately __ Very much __ Extremely
PB21. [*TELEPHONE: The next one is*] Have behavioral health technicians become certified trainers for military resilience, prevention, and non-medical wellness programs that are implemented outside the Military Health System	__ Not at all __ Slightly __ Moderately __ Very much __ Extremely
PB22. [*TELEPHONE: The next one is*] Prepare behavioral health technicians to work in geographic locations in which they are physically separated from their supervising provider (e.g., receiving video or electronic supervision)	__ Not at all __ Slightly __ Moderately __ Very much __ Extremely

Satisfaction

Taking all things into consideration, how satisfied are you, in general, with each of the following aspects of being in the military?[2]

S1. The type of work you do in your military job	__ Very satisfied __ Satisfied __ Neither satisfied nor dissatisfied __ Dissatisfied __ Very dissatisfied
S2. The quality of your supervisor	__ Very satisfied __ Satisfied __ Neither satisfied nor dissatisfied __ Dissatisfied __ Very dissatisfied

Please indicate how strongly you agree with the following statements.[3]

S3. My personality is a good match for this job.	__ Strongly disagree __ Disagree __ Somewhat disagree __ Neither disagree nor agree __ Somewhat agree __ Agree __ Strongly agree

[2] The following questions were adapted from the 2017 SOFS (see U.S. Department of Defense, Office of People Analytics, 2017).

[3] The following questions were adapted from Lauver and Kristof-Brown, 2001.

S4. I am the right type of person for this type of work	__ Strongly disagree
	__ Disagree
	__ Somewhat disagree
	__ Neither disagree nor agree
	__ Somewhat agree
	__ Agree
	__ Strongly agree

Provider Attributes

This last set of questions requests important background and demographic information that will help us to describe the group of respondents to this survey.[4]

PRA1. Are you of Hispanic or Latino origin or descent?	__ No
	__ Yes
	__ Prefer not to answer
	[PROGRAMMING NOTE: Display on web version.]
	[TELEPHONE NOTE: Do not read this item. Select only if the respondent indicates that they would prefer not to answer.]

---

[4] The following questions were adapted from Hepner et al., 2017.

PRA2. [WEB] What is your race? Please select one or more. [TELEPHONE] What is your race? Please choose all that apply.	__ White __ Black or African American __ Asian __ Native Hawaiian or other Pacific Islander __ American Indian or Alaskan Native __ None of these (please describe): _____ __ Prefer not to answer

PRA3. [WEB] Please indicate your military status. [TELEPHONE] Which of the following best describes your military status. Are you . . .	__ Active component __ National Guard __ Reserve __ DoD civilian __ Other (please describe): _____

PRA4. What service branch do you work in?	__ Army __ Navy __ Air Force

[WEB]
Thank you for completing our survey. As a token of appreciation, we are able to send you a $50 gift card via email if you completed this survey during off-duty time.

Which $50 gift card would you like to receive?
__ $50 Amazon gift card
__ $50 Starbucks gift card
__ I would like to decline the gift card.

The gift card will come directly to your email. What email address should we send it to? We will only use that email for the purposes of sending you the gift card.

Email address: _____
__ Prefer not to provide email and forgo the gift card.

[TELEPHONE]
Thank you for completing our survey. As a token of appreciation, we are able to send you a $50 gift card via email if you completed this survey during off-duty time.

Which $50 gift card would you like to receive?
__ $50 Amazon gift card
__ $50 Starbucks gift card
__ Respondent declined gift card.

The gift card will come directly to your email. What email address should we send it to? We will only use that email for the purposes of sending you the gift card.

Email address: _____
__ Prefer not to provide email and forgo the gift card.

[CLOSING/THANK YOU TEXT]
Thank you for taking the time to complete this survey. Your responses provide important insight into the experiences of behavioral health technicians within the Military Health System.

We would be happy to answer any questions you might have about the study or your participation. For more information about this survey, you may contact

Kimberly Hepner, Ph.D.
Senior Behavioral Scientist, RAND Corporation
Tel: (310) 393-0411 ext. 6381
Email: Kimberly_Hepner@rand.org

MHP Survey

Informed Consent

[TELEPHONE] Before we begin, I need to read through some important and relevant information regarding this study. Though we already briefly touched on some of these details, the information that I'll review will make sure you have a complete understanding of this study and its purpose.

[WEB TITLE] Optimizing the Role of Military Behavioral Health Technicians

[TELEPHONE INTRO] You have been invited to participate in a survey about experiences working with uniformed behavioral health technicians. Behavioral health technicians are also referred to as L24A or psych techs in the Navy; behavioral health specialists or Sixty-Eight X-Rays in the Army; or mental health technicians or Four Charlies in the Air Force. For the remainder of the survey, we use the term "behavioral health technician" to describe this occupation. Through this survey, we aim to learn about the roles and skills of behavioral health technicians, their training and supervision, along with ways that the roles of behavioral health technicians could be expanded or changed.

[WEB INTRO] You have been invited to participate in a survey about your experiences working with uniformed behavioral health technicians (L24A), behavioral health specialists (68X), or mental health technicians (4C0X1). For the remainder of the survey, we will be using the term "behavioral health technician" to describe this occupation. Through this survey, we aim to learn about the roles and skills of behavioral health technicians, their

training and supervision, along with ways that the roles of behavioral health technicians could be expanded or changed.

[*TELEPHONE AND WEB*] The RAND Corporation, a private, nonprofit research institution, is conducting this research project, which is funded by the Department of Defense (DoD) through the Psychological Health Center of Excellence. Davis Research is working with RAND to conduct the survey.

The survey will take approximately 25 minutes to complete online, or 30 minutes if you complete it by telephone. While there is no direct benefit to you for participation in this research project, our findings could help to optimize the use of behavioral health technicians within the Military Health System (MHS). If you complete the survey during off-duty time, we will provide a $50 gift card as a token of appreciation. You may complete the survey during duty time, if you decline the gift card incentive.

Your participation in this survey is entirely voluntary. If you do decide to participate, you can skip questions or stop taking the survey at any time. Choosing not to participate or not to answer some questions will not result in any penalty.

Disclosure of survey responses could cause personal or professional embarrassment. However, the risk of disclosure is minimal due to the difficulty in identifying individuals and the care that will be taken by the personnel who have access to the data. We will protect the confidentiality of your responses, and your supervisor will not have access to the information you provide. [*NEXT SENTENCE WEB ONLY*] Information you provide will not be linked to your email address or IP address. RAND will not include any participant names in any reports. The RAND Corporation's Human Subjects Protection Committee and the Defense Health Agency Headquarters Human Research Protection Program have reviewed and approved the study procedures. Representatives of DoD are authorized to review our research records.

The DoD Privacy Advisory states that the Defense Manpower Data Center has provided certain information about you to allow RAND to conduct this survey. Your name and contact information have been used to send you notifications and information about this survey. The Defense Manpower Data Center has provided certain demographic information to reduce the number of questions in the survey and minimize the burden on your time. Using a unique participant ID, your responses will be linked with these demographic data by RAND to allow for a thorough analysis of the responses. RAND has not been authorized by DoD to identify or link survey responses and demographic information with your name and contact information. The resulting reports will only include analysis of respondent groupings of 5 or more so that no individual could be identified.

We would be happy to answer any questions you might have about the study or your participation. For more information about this survey, you may contact:

Kimberly Hepner, Ph.D.
Senior Behavioral Scientist, RAND Corporation
Tel: (310) 393-0411 ext. 6381
Email: Kimberly_Hepner@rand.org

If you have questions about your rights as a research participant or need to report a research-related injury or concern, you can contact RAND's Human Subjects Protection Committee toll-free at (866) 697-5620 or by emailing hspcinfo@rand.org. If possible, when you contact the Committee, please reference Study #2018-0138.

This survey received all required human subjects and regulatory approvals. The survey Report Control Symbol (RCS) license number is DD-HA-2703 (Washington Headquarters Services).

[*WEB*] Please indicate whether you consent to participate in this study:
[*TELEPHONE*] Do you consent to participate in this study?

__ Yes, I agree to participate.
__ I do not want to participate in this study and I would like to exit the survey now.

Eligibility Screening

Before beginning, we need to see if this study applies to you and your work.

E1. [WEB] In the past year, have you worked with a uniformed behavioral health technician in a clinical setting? This could include supervising a behavioral health technician or providing clinical services with a behavioral health technician. Behavioral health technicians are also referred to as psych techs or L24A in the Navy; behavioral health specialists or 68X in the Army; or mental health technicians or 4C0X1 in the Air Force.

[TELEPHONE] In the past year, have you worked with a uniformed behavioral health technician in a clinical setting? This could include supervising a behavioral health technician or providing clinical services with a behavioral health technician. [TELEPHONE: Repeat this information for the respondent only as needed] Behavioral health technicians are also referred to as psych techs in the Navy; behavioral health specialists or Sixty-Eight X-Rays in the Army; or mental health technicians or Four Charlies in the Air Force.

___ Yes
___ No

[Require respondents to answer this question. Do NOT allow skip.]

[If the respondent is ineligible to participate]

Based on your response, you have not worked with a uniformed behavioral health technician, behavioral health specialist, or mental health technician in the past year. Since our study focuses on experiences working with individuals in this occupation, it does not appear that you are eligible to participate. Therefore, there are no further questions for you to answer.

Thank you again for your time and for your service to the military.

Thank you.

[If the respondent is eligible to participate]

You are eligible to participate in this survey.

[*WEB*] As you take the survey, please do not include any personally identifiable information in your responses. Any identifiable information inadvertently provided within the survey will be removed from the data and reporting of results.

[*TELEPHONE*] Please do not include any personally identifiable information with your responses. Any identifiable information inadvertently provided within the survey will be removed from the data and reporting of results.

Survey Items

Practice Attributes

[*For the remaining items, allow respondents to skip past them without answering the question. Unless otherwise specified in the coding instructions, skip to the next item. Display a message confirming that they intended to leave the question blank before continuing to next screen.*]

The first set of questions asks about your clinical experience and the settings in which you practice.

[*PROGRAMMING NOTE: Allow to enter year and not month. Display error message if months entered without years. Force years to 0 if >11 months entered.*]

PA1. How long have you practiced as a mental health clinician since **earning your highest degree?**[a] [*TELEPHONE: You can give your answer in years and months.*]	_____ years _____ months
PA2. How long have you practiced as a mental health clinician in the **Military Health System?** [*TELEPHONE: You can give your answer in years and months.*]	_____ years _____ months
[a] Question adapted from Hepner et al., 2017.	

PA3. Within the last month, in which settings have you spent time interacting with patients during duty hours? [*WEB: Please select all settings in which you currently work.*] [*TELEPHONE: I will quickly read a short list of possible options. Please let me know which ones apply to you in the last month.*]	__ Outpatient mental health (including intensive outpatient programs) __ Inpatient mental health __ Outpatient substance use __ Inpatient substance use __ Primary care __ Behavioral health (integrated mental health and substance use) __ Emergency department __ Other (please specify): _____ __ None
PA4. In the past 12 months, did you spend any time deployed, including both combat and non–combat zone deployments (excluding training missions)? This includes current deployments.[a]	__ Yes __ No

[a] Question adapted from DoD Health Related Behaviors Survey (see Meadows et al., 2021).

[*PROGRAMMING NOTE: If PA4 = "yes," proceed to PA5. If PA4 = "no," skip to RS1.*]

PA5. Did you work with a behavioral health technician while deployed? This could include supervising a behavioral health technician or providing clinical services with a behavioral health technician.	__ Yes __ No

Responsibilities and Skills

The next section asks about your role as a behavioral health provider.

RS1. Do you have a leadership position in your clinic (e.g., head of a clinic or clinical team)?	__ Yes __ No

For the next set of questions, we are interested in the set of duties and tasks that behavioral health technicians perform. For each of the following tasks, we will ask you how often behavioral health technicians perform the task, and how proficient behavioral health technicians are in performing the task.[1]

[WEB] For each item, please answer the following questions:

[TELEPHONE] For each item, you will be asked to answer the following two questions:

- How often do the behavioral health technicians you work with currently perform each of the following tasks?
- How proficient are behavioral health technicians in performing each task?

[WEB NOTE: Each item-specific screen should begin with the item as noted below, and have the following two questions:]

- How often do the behavioral health technicians you work with currently perform this task?
- How proficient are behavioral health technicians in performing this task?

[TELEPHONE: For each item, read the item, then ask:

---

[1]   In this set of questions, response options drew on Pynes, 2009, and Lytell et al., 2017.

- *(ITEM_F): Do the behavioral health technicians you work with currently perform this task [READ OPTIONS]?*
- *(ITEM_P) How proficient are the behavioral health technicians you work with in performing this task? Would you say . . . (read options)]?*

[TELEPHONE NOTE: Please read the text in parentheses for each question. "i.e." should be read as "that is"; "e.g." should be read as "for example."]

The first set of questions will ask about screening and assessment.

RS2. [*TELEPHONE: The first task is*] Triage walk-in patients (i.e., briefly assess patient need and determine need for care)	RS2_F. Frequency: __ Never __ Rarely __ Sometimes __ Often __ Very often	RS2_P. Proficiency: __ They cannot perform this task. __ They can perform this task with assistance. __ They can perform this task with no assistance. __ They can perform this task with no assistance and they can train someone to perform this task.
RS3. Use the Behavioral Health Data Portal (BHDP)	RS3_F. Frequency: __ Never __ Rarely __ Sometimes __ Often __ Very often	RS3_P. Proficiency: __ They cannot perform this task. __ They can perform this task with assistance. __ They can perform this task with no assistance. __ They can perform this task with no assistance and they can train someone to perform this task.

RS4. Administer and score behavioral health symptom measures (e.g., PHQ-9, PCL, AUDIT-C)	RS4_F. Frequency: __ Never __ Rarely __ Sometimes __ Often __ Very often	RS4_P. Proficiency: __ They cannot perform this task. __ They can perform this task with assistance. __ They can perform this task with no assistance. __ They can perform this task with no assistance and they can train someone to perform this task.
RS5. Perform intake interviews/ evaluations (e.g., history of current problem)	RS5_F. Frequency: __ Never __ Rarely __ Sometimes __ Often __ Very often	RS5_P. Proficiency: __ They cannot perform this task. __ They can perform this task with assistance. __ They can perform this task with no assistance. __ They can perform this task with no assistance and they can train someone to perform this task.
RS6. Administer and score psychological tests (e.g., MMPI)	RS6_F. Frequency: __ Never __ Rarely __ Sometimes __ Often __ Very often	RS6_P. Proficiency: __ They cannot perform this task. __ They can perform this task with assistance. __ They can perform this task with no assistance. __ They can perform this task with no assistance and they can train someone to perform this task.

RS7. Administer and score cognitive and neuropsychological tests (e.g., RBANS, WAIS)	RS7_F. Frequency: __ Never __ Rarely __ Sometimes __ Often __ Very often	RS7_P. Proficiency: __ They cannot perform this task. __ They can perform this task with assistance. __ They can perform this task with no assistance. __ They can perform this task with no assistance and they can train someone to perform this task.
RS8. Perform risk assessments (e.g., suicide risk, homicide risk)	RS8_F. Frequency: __ Never __ Rarely __ Sometimes __ Often __ Very often	RS8_P. Proficiency: __ They cannot perform this task. __ They can perform this task with assistance. __ They can perform this task with no assistance. __ They can perform this task with no assistance and they can train someone to perform this task.

The next set of questions will ask about psychosocial interventions.

RS9. [*TELEPHONE: The first task is*] Provide supportive counseling for mental health concerns	RS9_F. Frequency: __ Never __ Rarely __ Sometimes __ Often __ Very often	RS9_P. Proficiency: __ They cannot perform this task. __ They can perform this task with assistance. __ They can perform this task with no assistance. __ They can perform this task with no assistance and they can train someone to perform this task.
RS10. Provide supportive counseling for substance use disorders or alcohol or drug use concerns	RS10_F. Frequency: __ Never __ Rarely __ Sometimes __ Often __ Very often	RS10_P. Proficiency: __ They cannot perform this task. __ They can perform this task with assistance. __ They can perform this task with no assistance. __ They can perform this task with no assistance and they can train someone to perform this task.
RS11. Deliver specific evidence-based psychotherapy for mental health concerns (e.g., cognitive behavioral therapy for depression)	RS11_F. Frequency: __ Never __ Rarely __ Sometimes __ Often __ Very often	RS11_P. Proficiency: __ They cannot perform this task. __ They can perform this task with assistance. __ They can perform this task with no assistance. __ They can perform this task with no assistance and they can train someone to perform this task.

RS12. Deliver specific evidence-based psychotherapy for substance use disorders (e.g., cognitive behavioral relapse prevention therapy)	RS12_F. Frequency: __ Never __ Rarely __ Sometimes __ Often __ Very often	RS12_P. Proficiency: __ They cannot perform this task. __ They can perform this task with assistance. __ They can perform this task with no assistance. __ They can perform this task with no assistance and they can train someone to perform this task.
RS13. Facilitate group counseling or group therapy sessions	RS13_F. Frequency: __ Never __ Rarely __ Sometimes __ Often __ Very often	RS13_P. Proficiency: __ They cannot perform this task. __ They can perform this task with assistance. __ They can perform this task with no assistance. __ They can perform this task with no assistance and they can train someone to perform this task.
RS14. Facilitate psychoeducational groups (e.g., stress management, smoking cessation)	RS14_F. Frequency: __ Never __ Rarely __ Sometimes __ Often __ Very often	RS14_P. Proficiency: __ They cannot perform this task. __ They can perform this task with assistance. __ They can perform this task with no assistance. __ They can perform this task with no assistance and they can train someone to perform this task.

The next set of questions will ask about case management.

RS15. [*TELEPHONE: The first task is*] Develop treatment plans	RS15_F. Frequency: __ Never __ Rarely __ Sometimes __ Often __ Very often	RS15_P. Proficiency: __ They cannot perform this task. __ They can perform this task with assistance. __ They can perform this task with no assistance. __ They can perform this task with no assistance and they can train someone to perform this task.
RS16. Review patient homework (e.g., between session activities or logs)	RS16_F. Frequency: __ Never __ Rarely __ Sometimes __ Often __ Very often	RS16_P. Proficiency: __ They cannot perform this task. __ They can perform this task with assistance. __ They can perform this task with no assistance. __ They can perform this task with no assistance and they can train someone to perform this task.

RS17. Perform case management activities (e.g., care coordination, referrals)	RS17_F. Frequency: __ Never __ Rarely __ Sometimes __ Often __ Very often	RS17_P. Proficiency: __ They cannot perform this task. __ They can perform this task with assistance. __ They can perform this task with no assistance. __ They can perform this task with no assistance and they can train someone to perform this task.
RS18. Monitor patient progress during treatment over time using symptom measures (e.g., PHQ-9, PCL, GAD-7)	RS18_F. Frequency: __ Never __ Rarely __ Sometimes __ Often __ Very often	RS18_P. Proficiency: __ They cannot perform this task. __ They can perform this task with assistance. __ They can perform this task with no assistance. __ They can perform this task with no assistance and they can train someone to perform this task.
RS19. Assess medication adherence and side effects	RS19_F. Frequency: __ Never __ Rarely __ Sometimes __ Often __ Very often	RS19_P. Proficiency: __ They cannot perform this task. __ They can perform this task with assistance. __ They can perform this task with no assistance. __ They can perform this task with no assistance and they can train someone to perform this task.

The next set of questions will ask about outreach and resilience activities.

RS20. [*TELEPHONE: The first task is*] Conduct behavioral health outreach to units or base community to provide information about behavioral health services	RS20_F. Frequency: __ Never __ Rarely __ Sometimes __ Often __ Very often	RS20_P. Proficiency: __ They cannot perform this task. __ They can perform this task with assistance. __ They can perform this task with no assistance. __ They can perform this task with no assistance and they can train someone to perform this task.
RS21. Conduct combat stress briefings, trainings, or interventions (e.g., Combat Operational Stress Control [COSC])	RS21_F. Frequency: __ Never __ Rarely __ Sometimes __ Often __ Very often	RS21_P. Proficiency: __ They cannot perform this task. __ They can perform this task with assistance. __ They can perform this task with no assistance. __ They can perform this task with no assistance and they can train someone to perform this task.

RS22. Conduct community prevention, intervention, or outreach briefings to units or base community	RS22_F. Frequency: __ Never __ Rarely __ Sometimes __ Often __ Very often	RS22_P. Proficiency: __ They cannot perform this task. __ They can perform this task with assistance. __ They can perform this task with no assistance. __ They can perform this task with no assistance and they can train someone to perform this task.
RS23. Provide behavioral health consultation in non-behavioral health clinical settings (e.g., in a medical or surgical setting)	RS23_F. Frequency: __ Never __ Rarely __ Sometimes __ Often __ Very often	RS23_P. Proficiency: __ They cannot perform this task. __ They can perform this task with assistance. __ They can perform this task with no assistance. __ They can perform this task with no assistance and they can train someone to perform this task.

RS24. Have you ever observed behavioral health technicians performing a task that you perceived to be outside their scope of practice? [TELEPHONE, IF YES: Was that only in deployed settings, only in garrison, or in both settings?]	__ Yes, only in deployed settings __ Yes, only in garrison __ Yes, in deployed settings and in garrison __ No

[PROGRAMMING NOTE: If any yes response above, ask RS24a. If no, skip to SCT1.]

RS24a. Please describe these tasks in as much detail as possible. ***Do not enter personally identifiable information.***	(Free response box)

Supervision, Collaboration, and Training

The next set of questions assesses your perceptions of the training and supervision that behavioral health technicians receive.

[*WEB*] Please rate your perceptions about the time behavioral health technicians spend in each of the following training activities.

[*TELEPHONE*] Please answer each item with "spend too much time," "spend too little time," "spent about the right amount of time," or "don't know."

SCT1. Classroom instruction at METC	__ Spend too much time __ Spend too little time __ Spend about the right amount of time __ Don't know
SCT2. Clinical practicum experience at METC	__ Spend too much time __ Spend too little time __ Spend about the right amount of time __ Don't know
SCT3. On-the-job training	__ Spend too much time __ Spend too little time __ Spend about the right amount of time __ Don't know

SCT4. Continuing education	__ Spend too much time
	__ Spend too little time
	__ Spend about the right amount of time
	__ Don't know

SCT5. Currently, do you provide clinical supervision to behavioral health technicians?[a]	__ Yes
	__ No
SCT6. At this time, do you feel like behavioral health technicians receive adequate supervision to perform their clinical duties?[a]	__ Yes
	__ No
	__ Unsure

[a] Question adapted from Stratton, 2014.

Perceptions of and Barriers to Effective BHT Practice

The next questions assess your perceptions of behavioral health technicians and their roles within the Military Health System.

[WEB] Please indicate your level of agreement with the following statements:

[TELEPHONE] Please tell me to what extent you agree with each of the following statements. For each statement, please answer "strongly disagree," "disagree," "neither disagree nor agree," "agree," or "strongly agree."

[TELEPHONE NOTE: Read response options for the first 2–3 items and then as needed.]

PB1. Licensed mental health providers are not familiar with the range of clinical activities behavioral health technicians are trained to provide.	__ Strongly disagree __ Disagree __ Neither disagree nor agree __ Agree __ Strongly agree
PB2. Licensed mental health providers who were trained more recently are less comfortable relying on behavioral health technicians.	__ Strongly disagree __ Disagree __ Neither disagree nor agree __ Agree __ Strongly agree
PB3. Civilian licensed mental health providers are less familiar than uniformed licensed mental health providers with the clinical tasks that behavioral health technicians are trained to perform.	__ Strongly disagree __ Disagree __ Neither disagree nor agree __ Agree __ Strongly agree
PB4. Licensed mental health providers have limited time to invest in ongoing supervision and training of behavioral health technicians.	__ Strongly disagree __ Disagree __ Neither disagree nor agree __ Agree __ Strongly agree
PB5. Behavioral health technicians need more systematic supervision to effectively provide clinical care.	__ Strongly disagree __ Disagree __ Neither disagree nor agree __ Agree __ Strongly agree

PB6. Licensed mental health providers would be more comfortable sharing clinical tasks with behavioral health technicians if they had a credential (e.g., Certified Alcohol and Drug Counselor [CADC]).	__ Strongly disagree __ Disagree __ Neither disagree nor agree __ Agree __ Strongly agree
PB7. Behavioral health technicians are primarily needed to cover the administrative responsibilities in clinics.	__ Strongly disagree __ Disagree __ Neither disagree nor agree __ Agree __ Strongly agree
PB8. Behavioral health technicians have limited dedicated time spent in clinical settings due to other unit responsibilities.	__ Strongly disagree __ Disagree __ Neither disagree nor agree __ Agree __ Strongly agree
PB9. If licensed mental health providers integrate behavioral health technicians more into clinical care, they won't get "credit" for delivering the care (i.e., it won't help their RVUs).	__ Strongly disagree __ Disagree __ Neither disagree nor agree __ Agree __ Strongly agree
PB10. There can be substantial variability in behavioral health technician skills, even within the same rank.	__ Strongly disagree __ Disagree __ Neither disagree nor agree __ Agree __ Strongly agree

PB11. Behavioral health technicians would feel more comfortable receiving on-the-job training from a senior enlisted behavioral health technician than from a licensed mental health provider.	__ Strongly disagree __ Disagree __ Neither disagree nor agree __ Agree __ Strongly agree

The next set of statements describe potential changes for behavioral health technicians or the licensed mental health providers who work with them.

[WEB] Please indicate the extent to which each option would enable behavioral health technicians to be more effective within the Military Health System.

[TELEPHONE] To what extent would each of the following options enable behavioral health technicians to be more effective within the Military Health System? For each item, please answer "not at all," "slightly," "moderately," "very much," or "extremely."

[TELEPHONE NOTE: Read response options for the first 2–3 items and then as needed.]

PB13. Establish specific training plans for behavioral health technicians upon leaving the METC ("The Schoolhouse")	__ Not at all __ Slightly __ Moderately __ Very much __ Extremely
PB14. Provide templates, checklists, or forms to structure clinical tasks (e.g., clinical interviews) for behavioral health technicians	__ Not at all __ Slightly __ Moderately __ Very much __ Extremely

PB15. Provide education to licensed mental health providers on how they can utilize behavioral health technicians	__ Not at all __ Slightly __ Moderately __ Very much __ Extremely
PB16. Establish administrative policies to better define components of behavioral health technician work (e.g., expectations for roles, supervision)	__ Not at all __ Slightly __ Moderately __ Very much __ Extremely
PB17. Train behavioral health technicians to implement treatment approaches that are effective across multiple psychiatric diagnoses (e.g., problem-solving therapy)	__ Not at all __ Slightly __ Moderately __ Very much __ Extremely
PB18. Train behavioral health technicians to implement evidence-based psychotherapies for lower risk patients (e.g., cognitive behavioral therapy for depression)	__ Not at all __ Slightly __ Moderately __ Very much __ Extremely
PB19. Train behavioral health technicians to implement evidence-based psychotherapies for more complex patients (e.g., cognitive processing therapy for PTSD)	__ Not at all __ Slightly __ Moderately __ Very much __ Extremely

PB20. Provide behavioral health technicians with opportunities to participate in ongoing professional development (e.g., courses through Army Medical Department Center and School, obtaining civilian credentials)	__ Not at all __ Slightly __ Moderately __ Very much __ Extremely
PB21. Have behavioral health technicians become certified trainers for military resilience, prevention, and non-medical wellness programs that are implemented outside the Military Health System	__ Not at all __ Slightly __ Moderately __ Very much __ Extremely
PB22. Prepare behavioral health technicians to work in geographic locations in which they are physically separated from their supervising provider (e.g., receiving video or electronic supervision)	__ Not at all __ Slightly __ Moderately __ Very much __ Extremely

Satisfaction

Taking all things into consideration, how satisfied are you, in general, with each of the following aspects of working in the military?

S1. In general, how satisfied are you with the performance of behavioral health technicians?	__ Very satisfied __ Somewhat satisfied __ Neither satisfied nor dissatisfied __ Somewhat dissatisfied __ Very dissatisfied

S2. The type of work you do in your military job?[a]	__ Very satisfied __ Satisfied __ Neither satisfied nor dissatisfied __ Dissatisfied __ Very dissatisfied
S3. The quality of your supervisor?[a]	__ Very satisfied __ Satisfied __ Neither satisfied nor dissatisfied __ Dissatisfied __ Very dissatisfied

[a] Question adapted from the 2017 SOFS (see U.S. Department of Defense, Office of People Analytics, 2017).

Provider Attributes

This last set of questions requests important background and demographic information that will help us to describe the group of respondents to this survey.[2]

PRA1. Are you of Hispanic or Latino origin or descent?	__ No __ Yes __ Prefer not to answer

---

[2] The following questions were adapted from Hepner et al., 2017.

PRA2. [WEB] What is your race? Please select one or more. [TELEPHONE] What is your race? Please choose all that apply.	__ White __ Black or African American __ Asian __ Native Hawaiian or other Pacific Islander __ American Indian or Alaskan Native __ None of these (please describe): _____ __ Prefer not to answer

PRA3. [WEB] Please indicate your military status. [TELEPHONE] Which of the following best describes your military status. Are you . . .	__ Active component __ National Guard __ Reserve __ DoD civilian __ Other (please describe): _____

PRA4. What service branch do you work in?	__ Army __ Navy __ Air Force __ Marine Corps __ Other (please describe): _____

PRA5. Are you a . . .	__ Clinical psychologist (Ph.D. or Psy.D.)
	__ Licensed clinical social worker (LCSW or MCSW)
	__ Master's-level, licensed professional counselor (e.g., LPC or LMHC)
	__ Psychiatrist (M.D. or D.O.), psychiatric nurse practitioner
	__ Other (please describe): _____

[*WEB*]

Thank you for completing our survey. As a token of appreciation, we are able to send you a $50 gift card via email if you completed this survey during off-duty time.

Which $50 gift card would you like to receive?
__ $50 Amazon gift card
__ $50 Starbucks gift card
__ I would like to decline the gift card.

The gift card will come directly to your email. What email address should we send it to? We will only use that email for the purposes of sending you the gift card.

Email address: _____
__ Prefer not to provide email and forgo the gift card.

[*TELEPHONE*]

Thank you for completing our survey. As a token of appreciation, we are able to send you a $50 gift card via email if you completed this survey during off-duty time.

Which $50 gift card would you like to receive?

__ $50 Amazon gift card
__ $50 Starbucks gift card
__ Respondent declined gift card.

The gift card will come directly to your email. What email address should we send it to? We will only use that email for the purposes of sending you the gift card.

Email address: _____
__ Prefer not to provide email and forgo the gift card.

[CLOSING/THANK YOU TEXT]
Thank you for taking the time to complete this survey. Your responses provide important insight into the experiences of behavioral health technicians within the Military Health System.

Supplementary Analyses

This appendix includes figures and tables that supplement the analyses presented in Chapters Four through Nine:

- Figures E.1 and E.2 provide additional detail on the findings presented in Chapter Four.
- Figures E.3 and E.4 provide additional detail on the findings presented in Chapter Five.
- Figure E.5 provides additional detail on the findings presented in Chapter Six.
- Figures E.6 and E.7 and Tables E.1–E.6 provide additional detail on the findings presented in Chapter Seven.
- Figures E.8–E.10 provide additional detail on the findings presented in Chapter Eight.
- Tables E.7–E.12 and Figures E.11–E.12 provide additional detail on the findings presented in Chapter Nine.

FIGURE E.1
Frequency with Which BHTs Reported Performing Clinical Tasks

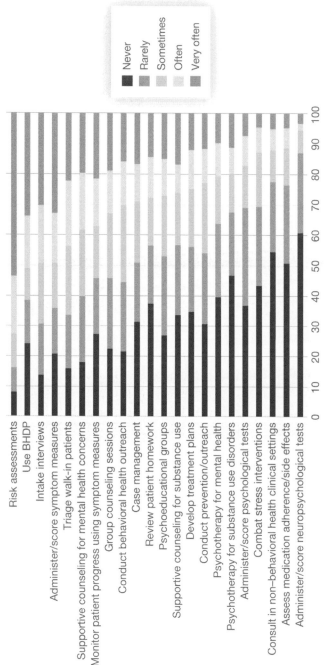

NOTE: *n* = 527–530.

FIGURE E.2

MHP-Reported Frequency with Which BHTs Performed Clinical Tasks

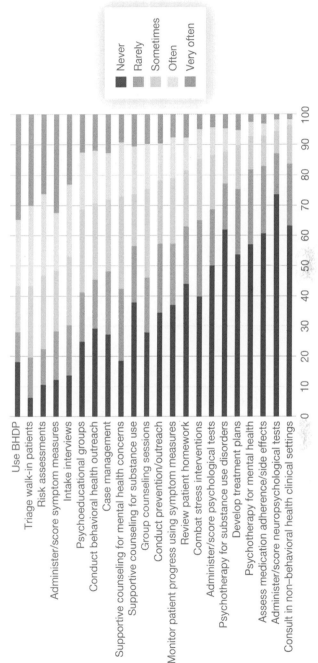

NOTE: n = 651–659.

FIGURE E.3

BHT Self-Reported Proficiency in Performing Clinical Tasks

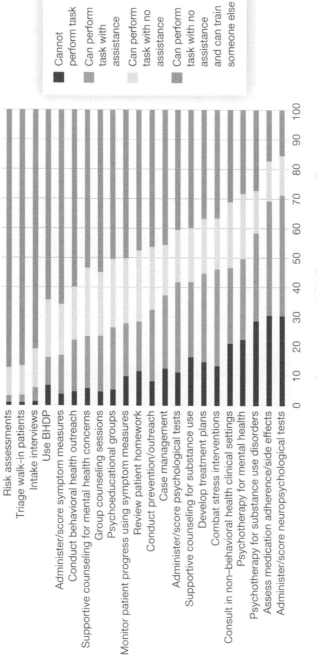

NOTE: n = 517–527.

FIGURE E.4

MHP-Reported BHT Proficiency in Performing Clinical Tasks

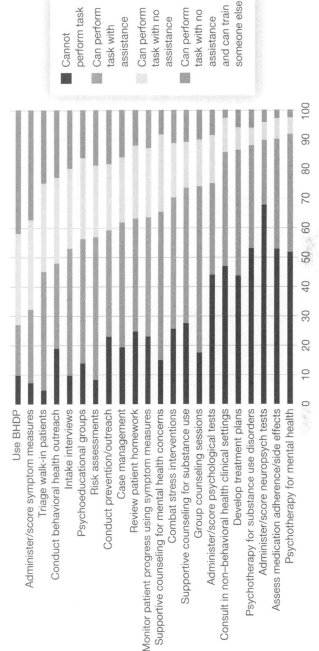

NOTE: *n* = 593–663.

FIGURE E.5

BHT and MHP Perceptions of Supervision Adequacy, Overall and by Service Branch

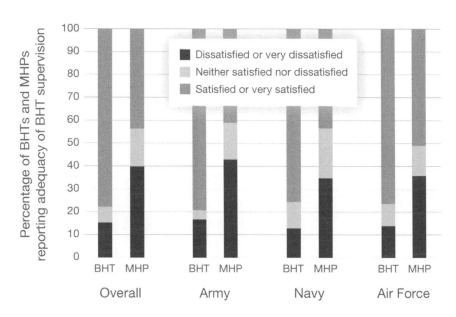

NOTES: BHTs: n = 526; MHPs: n = 657.

FIGURE E.6
BHT Perceptions of Barriers to Effective BHT Practice

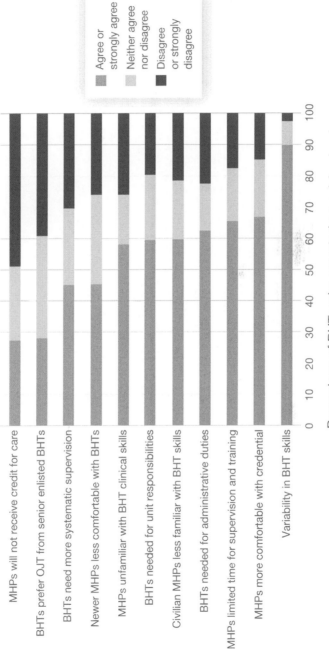

NOTE: *n* = 525–526.

TABLE E.1

BHT Perceptions of Barriers to Effective BHT Practice, by Service Branch

Barrier	Army (%)	Navy (%)	Air Force (%)
Licensed MHPs are not familiar with the range of clinical activities BHTs are trained to provide	54.4	65.0	61.0
Licensed MHPs who were trained more recently are less comfortable relying on BHTs***	48.3[a]	63.8[b]	36.8[c]
Civilian licensed MHPs are less familiar than uniformed licensed MHPs with the clinical tasks that BHTs are trained to perform	52.1	70.4	66.8
Licensed MHPs have limited time to invest in ongoing supervision and training of BHTs*	59.0[a]	73.2[ab]	71.8[b]
BHTs need more-systematic supervision to effectively provide clinical care**	37.5[a]	41.2[a]	56.4[b]
Licensed MHPs would be more comfortable sharing clinical tasks with BHTs if they had a credential**	73.1[a]	68.0[a]	58.6[b]
BHTs are primarily needed to cover the administrative responsibilities in clinics*	57.6[ab]	55.5[b]	70.6[a]
BHTs have limited dedicated time spent in clinical settings due to other unit responsibilities***	53.9[a]	44.8[a]	71.0[b]
If licensed MHPs integrate BHTs more into clinical care, they won't get "credit" for delivering the care	25.9	29.8	28.8
There can be substantial variability in BHTs' skills, even within the same rank**	86.2[a]	92.5[b]	93.6[b]
BHTs would feel more comfortable receiving OJT from a senior enlisted BHT than from a licensed MHP	28.8	30.9	26.2

NOTES: * $p < 0.05$, ** $p < 0.01$, *** $p < 0.001$. Values with differing letter superscripts within rows are statistically different at the $p < 0.05$ level, according to post hoc paired comparisons. $n = 525–526$.

TABLE E.2

BHT Perceptions of Barriers to Effective BHT Practice, by Time in Practice

Barrier	0–2 Years (%)	2–7 Years (%)	More Than 7 Years (%)
Licensed MHPs are not familiar with the range of clinical activities BHTs are trained to provide***	37.4[a]	58.3[b]	71.9[c]
Licensed MHPs who were trained more recently are less comfortable relying on BHTs***	33.1[a]	46.4[b]	52.6[b]
Civilian licensed MHPs are less familiar than uniformed licensed MHPs with the clinical tasks that BHTs are trained to perform***	34.4[a]	58.0[b]	79.7[c]
Licensed MHPs have limited time to invest in ongoing supervision and training of BHTs***	49.9[a]	68.0[b]	72.8[b]
BHTs need more systematic supervision to effectively provide clinical care***	25.7[a]	41.9[b]	63.3[c]
Licensed MHPs would be more comfortable sharing clinical tasks with BHTs if they had a credential**	56.4[a]	65.2[a]	76.4[b]
BHTs are primarily needed to cover the administrative responsibilities in clinics	58.0	66.5	59.9
BHTs have limited dedicated time spent in clinical settings due to other unit responsibilities	53.6	59.3	64.1
If licensed MHPs further integrate BHTs into clinical care, they won't get "credit" for delivering the care	20.2	27.4	32.5
There can be substantial variability in BHTs' skills, even within the same rank***	79.8[a]	90.9[b]	95.0[c]
BHTs would feel more comfortable receiving OJT from a senior enlisted BHT than from a licensed MHP	30.4	28.4	26.0

NOTES: ** $p < 0.01$, *** $p < 0.001$. Values with differing letter superscripts within rows are statistically different at the $p < 0.05$ level, according to post hoc paired comparisons. $n = 525–526$.

FIGURE E.7
MHP Perceptions of Barriers to Effective BHT Practice

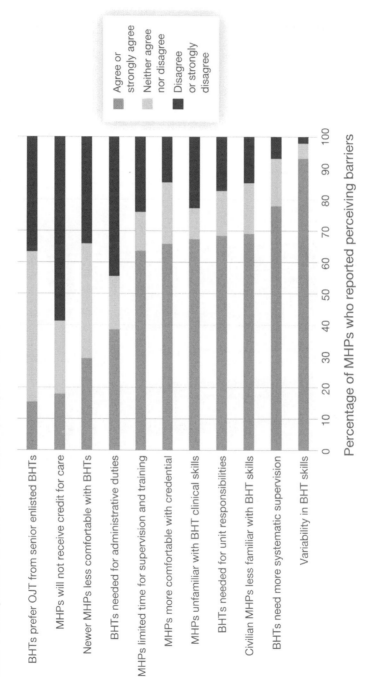

NOTE: $n = 652–656$

TABLE E.3

MHP Perceptions of Barriers to Effective BHT Practice, by Service Branch

Barrier	Army (%)	Navy (%)	Air Force (%)
Licensed MHPs are not familiar with the range of clinical activities BHTs are trained to provide	67.8	75.3	60.4
Licensed MHPs who were trained more recently are less comfortable relying on BHTs	27.5	37.5	28.3
Civilian licensed MHPs are less familiar than uniformed licensed MHPs with the clinical tasks that BHTs are trained to perform	67.9	67.7	72.9
Licensed MHPs have limited time to invest in ongoing supervision and training of BHTs	61.1	66.9	68.2
BHTs need more systematic supervision to effectively provide clinical care	80.8	66.8	78.0
Licensed MHPs would be more comfortable sharing clinical tasks with BHTs if they had a credential*	62.7[a]	64.8[a]	75.3[b]
BHTs are primarily needed to cover the administrative responsibilities in clinics	37.3	37.3	42.7
BHTs have limited dedicated time spent in clinical settings due to other unit responsibilities*	72.9[a]	58.8[b]	63.8[b]
If licensed MHPs integrate BHTs more into clinical care, they won't get "credit" for delivering the care	18.7	14.6	18.1
There can be substantial variability in BHTs' skills, even within the same rank	93.9	94.0	90.8
BHTs would feel more comfortable receiving OJT from a senior enlisted BHT than from a licensed MHP**	12.7[a]	18.1[a]	20.6[b]

NOTES: * $p < 0.05$, ** $p < 0.01$. Values with differing letter superscripts within rows are statistically different at the $p < 0.05$ level, according to post hoc paired comparisons. $n = 652–656$.

TABLE E.4
MHP Perceptions of Barriers to Effective BHT Practice, by Provider Type

Barrier	Psychiatrist or Psychiatric Nurse Practitioner (%)	Doctoral-Level Psychologist (%)	Master's-Level Clinician (%)
Licensed MHPs are not familiar with the range of clinical activities BHTs are trained to provide*	77.3[a]	70.4[b]	62.4[b]
Licensed MHPs who were trained more recently are less comfortable relying on BHTs	37.1	27.5	27.4
Civilian licensed MHPs are less familiar than uniformed licensed MHPs with the clinical tasks that BHTs are trained to perform	70.0	71.6	67.5
Licensed MHPs have limited time to invest in ongoing supervision and training of BHTs*	70.3[a]	72.4[a]	57.1[b]
BHTs need more systematic supervision to effectively provide clinical care*	70.8[a]	81.1[b]	78.8[ab]
Licensed MHPs would be more comfortable sharing clinical tasks with BHTs if they had a credential	67.6	72.7	62.2
BHTs are primarily needed to cover the administrative responsibilities in clinics	35.4	36.5	40.6
BHTs have limited dedicated time spent in clinical settings due to other unit responsibilities	69.6	64.3	70.1
If licensed MHPs integrate BHTs more into clinical care, they won't get "credit" for delivering the care	16.0	17.3	18.8
There can be substantial variability in BHTs' skills, even within the same rank***	95.2[a]	93.7[b]	92.2[a]
BHTs would feel more comfortable receiving OJT from a senior enlisted BHT than from a licensed MHP	21.4	11.4	15.2

NOTES: * $p < 0.05$, *** $p < 0.001$. Values with differing letter superscripts within rows are statistically different at the $p < 0.05$ level, according to post hoc paired comparisons. $n = 652$–656.

TABLE E.5

MHP Perceptions of Barriers to Effective BHT Practice, by Time in Practice in the MHS

Barrier	Years (%)			
	0–5	5–10	10–20	More than 20
Licensed MHPs are not familiar with the range of clinical activities BHTs are trained to provide	71.2	68.4	64.6	57.7
Licensed MHPs who were trained more recently are less comfortable relying on BHTs	32.2	34.4	22.4	22.2
Civilian licensed MHPs are less familiar than uniformed licensed MHPs with the clinical tasks that BHTs are trained to perform	71.7	70.3	66.9	61.4
Licensed MHPs have limited time to invest in ongoing supervision and training of BHTs	65.2	65.8	62.0	55.4
BHTs need more systematic supervision to effectively provide clinical care	74.5	85.1	75.2	73.7
Licensed MHPs would be more comfortable sharing clinical tasks with BHTs if they had a credential	69.0	67.7	61.3	62.9
BHTs are primarily needed to cover the administrative responsibilities in clinics	42.7	40.4	31.0	40.3
BHTs have limited dedicated time spent in clinical settings due to other unit responsibilities*	59.4[a]	71.5[b]	76.6[b]	66.1[ab]
If licensed MHPs integrate BHTs more into clinical care, they won't get "credit" for delivering the care	16.2	20.3	19.2	11.6
There can be substantial variability in BHTs' skills, even within the same rank	91.7	95.6	93.5	89.3
BHTs would feel more comfortable receiving OJT from a senior enlisted BHT than from a licensed MHP	19.8	15.0	6.5	29.1

NOTES: * $p < 0.05$. Values with differing letter superscripts within rows are statistically different at the $p < 0.05$ level, according to post hoc paired comparisons. $n = 652$–656.

TABLE E.6

MHP Perceptions of Barriers to Effective BHT Practice, by Military Status

Barrier	Active Duty (%)	Civilian (%)
Licensed MHPs are not familiar with the range of clinical activities BHTs are trained to provide	72.4	62.9
Licensed MHPs who were trained more recently are less comfortable relying on BHTs	34.4	24.8
Civilian licensed MHPs are less familiar than uniformed licensed MHPs with the clinical tasks that BHTs are trained to perform***	79.4[a]	59.9[b]
Licensed MHPs have limited time to invest in ongoing supervision and training of BHTs*	70.3[a]	57.8[b]
BHTs need more-systematic supervision to effectively provide clinical care	81.2	74.9
Licensed MHPs would be more comfortable sharing clinical tasks with BHTs if they had a credential	68.3	63.8
BHTs are primarily needed to cover the administrative responsibilities in clinics	37.7	39.3
BHTs have limited dedicated time spent in clinical settings due to other unit responsibilities	68.4	68.5
Licensed MHPs would be more comfortable sharing clinical care, they won't get "credit" for delivering the care***	12.6[a]	22.6[b]
There can be substantial variability in BHTs' skills, even within the same rank***	95.7[a]	91.0[b]
BHTs would feel more comfortable receiving OJT from a senior enlisted BHT than from a licensed MHP	14.5	16.2

NOTES: * $p < 0.05$, *** $p < 0.001$. Values with differing letter superscripts within rows are statistically different at the $p < 0.05$ level, according to post hoc paired comparisons. $n = 652$–656.

FIGURE E.8

BHT Satisfaction, Overall and by Service Branch

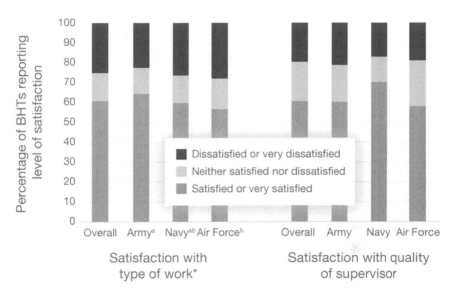

NOTES: * $p < 0.05$. Values with differing letter superscripts within column clusters are statistically different at the $p < 0.05$ level, according to post hoc paired comparisons. $n = 524$.

FIGURE E.9

BHT Satisfaction with Their Work, by Time Spent on Patient Care

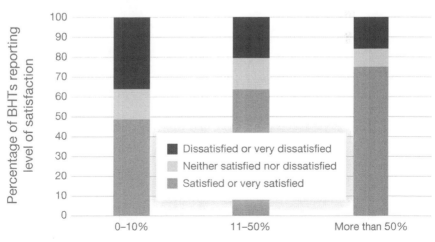

NOTE: $n = 489$.

FIGURE E.10

MHP Satisfaction with BHTs' Performance, Overall and by Service Branch

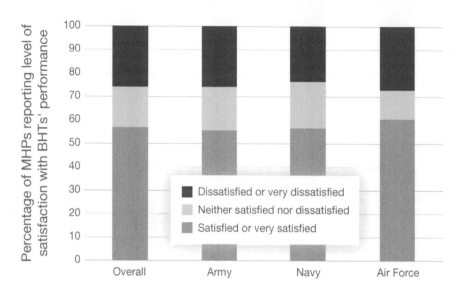

NOTE: *n* = 654.

TABLE E.7

BHT Perceptions of Potential Changes to BHT Practice, by Service Branch

Change to BHT Practice	Army (%)	Navy (%)	Air Force (%)
Establish specific training plans for BHTs upon leaving METC	58.3	58.2	52.2
Provide templates, checklists, or forms to structure clinical tasks for BHTs	62.4	61.3	57.1
Provide education to licensed MHPs on how they can utilize BHTs	78.1	84.1	76.3
Establish administrative policies to better define components of BHTs' work	71.0	79.9	68.5
Train BHTs to implement treatment approaches that are effective across multiple psychiatric diagnoses	80.4	88.1	82.5
Train BHTs to implement EBPs for lower-risk patients	81.1	91.4	82.1
Train BHTs to implement EBPs for more-complex patients*	72.9[ab]	80.5[a]	66.8[b]
Provide BHTs with opportunities to participate in ongoing professional development	90.8	95.0	88.6
Have BHTs become certified trainers for military resilience, prevention, and non-medical wellness programs that are implemented outside the MHS***	75.3[a]	84.5[a]	61.0[b]
Prepare BHTs to work in geographic locations in which they are physically separated from their supervising provider**	71.3[a]	75.5[a]	60.4[b]

NOTES: * $p < 0.05$, ** $p < 0.01$, *** $p < 0.001$. Values with differing letter superscripts within rows are statistically different at the $p < 0.05$ level, according to post hoc paired comparisons. $n = 524$–525.

FIGURE E.11

BHT Perceptions of Potential Changes to BHT Practice

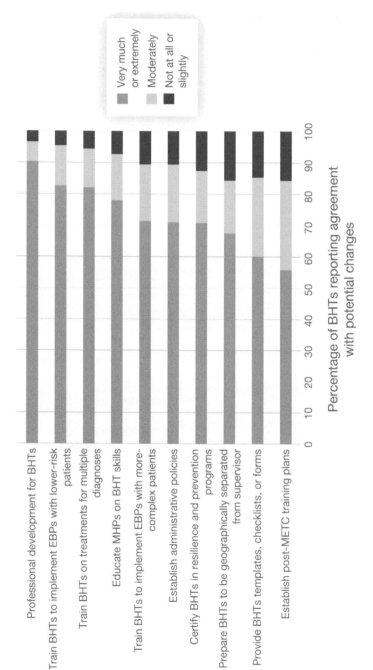

NOTE: n = 524–525.

TABLE E.8

BHT Perceptions of Potential Changes to BHT Practice, by Time in Practice

Change to BHT Practice	Years (%)		
	0–2	2–7	More Than 7
Establish specific training plans for BHTs upon leaving METC	59.8	54.6	55.2
Provide templates, checklists, or forms to structure clinical tasks for BHTs	67.1	59.7	56.1
Provide education to licensed MHPs on how they can utilize BHTs**	71.3[a]	76.6[a]	84.6[b]
Establish administrative policies to better define components of BHT work	73.4	67.4	74.3
Train BHTs to implement treatment approaches that are effective across multiple psychiatric diagnoses	80.8	79.4	86.5
Train BHTs to implement EBPs for lower-risk patients	81.4	80.0	86.9
Train BHTs to implement EBPs for more-complex patients	68.7	71.9	72.3
Provide BHTs with opportunities to participate in ongoing professional development	86.0	89.8	94.1
Have BHTs become certified trainers for military resilience, prevention, and non-medical wellness programs that are implemented outside the MHS	74.4	69.8	69.5
Prepare BHTs to work in geographic locations in which they are physically separated from their supervising provider**	69.9[a]	59.8[a]	76.4[b]

NOTES: ** $p < 0.01$. Values with differing letter superscripts within rows are statistically different at the $p < 0.05$ level, according to post hoc paired comparisons. $n = 524$–525.

FIGURE E.12
MHP Perceptions of Potential Changes to BHT Practice

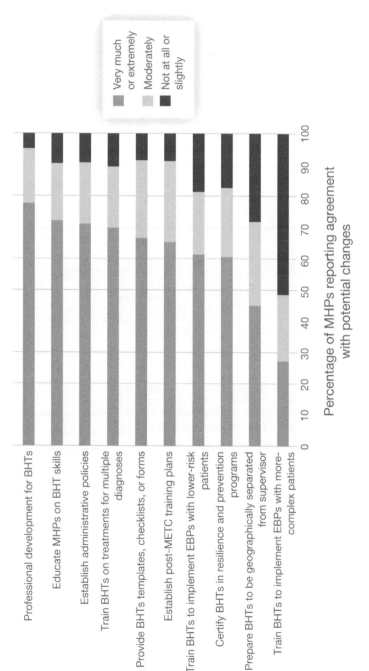

NOTE: n = 653–656.

TABLE E.9

MHP Perceptions of Potential Changes to BHT Practice, by Service Branch

Change to BHT Practice	Army (%)	Navy (%)	Air Force (%)
Establish specific training plans for BHTs upon leaving METC	64.4	72.7	63.5
Provide templates, checklists, or forms to structure clinical tasks for BHTs	68.2	68.6	61.2
Provide education to licensed MHPs on how they can utilize BHTs	71.1	73.8	74.0
Establish administrative policies to better define components of BHT work	72.0	76.6	65.8
Train BHTs to implement treatment approaches that are effective across multiple psychiatric diagnoses	69.3	73.7	68.9
Train BHTs to implement EBPs for lower-risk patients	58.4	64.2	67.8
Train BHTs to implement EBPs for more-complex patients	28.8	26.6	24.3
Provide BHTs with opportunities to participate in ongoing professional development	77.9	79.5	76.7
Have BHTs become certified trainers for military resilience, prevention, and non-medical wellness programs that are implemented outside the MHS	61.8	63.5	55.8
Prepare BHTs to work in geographic locations in which they are physically separated from their supervising provider	44.0	51.1	44.7

NOTE: n = 653–656.

TABLE E.10

MHP Perceptions of Potential Changes to BHT Practice, by Time in Practice in the MHS

Change to BHT Practice	Years (%)			
	0–5	5–10	10–20	More Than 20
Establish specific training plans for BHTs upon leaving METC	64.8	63.6	70.1	60.7
Provide templates, checklists, or forms to structure clinical tasks for BHTs	70.0	67.2	66.0	53.5
Provide education to licensed MHPs on how they can utilize BHTs	74.4	74.1	69.7	65.2
Establish administrative policies to better define components of BHT work*	69.3[a]	75.5[a]	73.7[a]	56.1[b]
Train BHTs to implement treatment approaches that are effective across multiple psychiatric diagnoses*	67.6[a]	73.5[a]	71.3[a]	61.7[b]
Train BHTs to implement EBPs for lower-risk patients**	64.7[a]	62.5[a]	61.5[a]	45.2[b]
Train BHTs to implement evidence-based psychotherapies for more complex patients	25.8	31.6	26.4	21.9
Provide BHTs with opportunities to participate in ongoing professional development	77.5	81.7	77.0	68.1
Have BHTs become certified trainers for military resilience, prevention, and non-medical wellness programs that are implemented outside the MHS	65.5	61.7	58.0	47.0
Prepare BHTs to work in geographic locations in which they are physically separated from their supervising provider	42.9	51.9	44.6	33.2

NOTES: * $p < 0.05$, ** $p < 0.01$. Values with differing letter superscripts within rows are statistically different at the $p < 0.05$ level, according to post hoc paired comparisons. $n = 653$–656.

TABLE E.11

MHP Perceptions of Potential Changes to BHT Practice, by Military Status

Change to BHT Practice	Active Duty (%)	Civilian (%)
Establish specific training plans for BHTs upon leaving METC	63.0	67.8
Provide templates, checklists, or forms to structure clinical tasks for BHTs	62.5	70.3
Provide education to licensed MHPs on how they can utilize BHTs	72.0	72.4
Establish administrative policies to better define components of BHT work	68.2	74.1
Train BHTs to implement treatment approaches that are effective across multiple psychiatric diagnoses***	75.3[a]	65.1b
Train BHTs to implement EBPs for lower-risk patients***	71.5[a]	52.6[b]
Train BHTs to implement EBPs for more-complex patients*	28.7[a]	26.3[b]
Provide BHTs with opportunities to participate in ongoing professional development*	77.5[a]	78.2[b]
Have BHTs become certified trainers for military resilience, prevention, and non-medical wellness programs that are implemented outside the MHS	60.2	61.1
Prepare BHTs to work in geographic locations in which they are physically separated from their supervising provider***	53.1[a]	38.4[b]

NOTES: * $p < 0.05$, ** $p < 0.01$, *** $p < 0.001$. Values with differing letter superscripts within rows are statistically different at the $p < 0.05$ level, according to post hoc paired comparisons. $n = 653–656$.

TABLE E.12
MHP Perceptions of Potential Changes to BHT Practice, by Provider Type

Change to BHT Practice	Psychiatrist or Psychiatric Nurse Practitioner (%)	Doctoral-Level Psychologist (%)	Master's-Level Clinician (%)
Establish specific training plans for BHTs upon leaving METC	67.8	62.3	66.3
Provide templates, checklists, or forms to structure clinical tasks for BHTs	60.9	65.3	69.3
Provide education to licensed MHPs on how they can utilize BHTs	74.0	64.2	75.4
Establish administrative policies to better define components of BHT work	68.1	69.7	73.2
Train BHTs to implement treatment approaches that are effective across multiple psychiatric diagnoses	66.9	70.4	70.7
Train BHTs to implement EBPs for lower-risk patients	57.2	61.0	63.3
Train BHTs to implement EBPs for more-complex patients**	27.1[a]	16.9[b]	32.5[a]
Provide BHTs with opportunities to participate in ongoing professional development*	68.7[a]	73.8[ab]	83.0[b]
Have BHTs become certified trainers for military resilience, prevention, and non-medical wellness programs that are implemented outside the MHS	60.6	56.6	62.7
Prepare BHTs to work in geographic locations in which they are physically separated from their supervising provider	45.6	50.9	42.5

NOTES: * $p < 0.05$, ** $p < 0.01$. Values with differing letter superscripts within rows are statistically different at the $p < 0.05$ level, according to post hoc paired comparisons. $n = 653$–656.

Abbreviations

BHDP	Behavioral Health Data Portal
BHT	behavioral health technician
BHTWG	Behavioral Health Technician Work Group
CADC	certified alcohol and drug counselor
DMDC	Defense Manpower Data Center
DoD	U.S. Department of Defense
EBP	evidence-based psychotherapy
METC	Medical Education and Training Campus
MHP	mental health provider
MHS	Military Health System
MMPI-2-RF	Minnesota Multiphasic Personality Inventory–2 Restructured Form
MTF	military treatment facility
OJT	on-the-job training
PHCoE	Psychological Health Center for Excellence
PTSD	posttraumatic stress disorder
RVU	relative value unit
SD	standard deviation
SOFS	Status of Forces Survey
TWANG	Toolkit for Weighting and Analysis of Nonequivalent Groups

References

Air Education and Training Command, *Course Training Plan L5ABJ4C031 01AA (PDS Code LBI) Mental Health Service Apprentice*, Randolph, Tex.: U.S. Air Force, 2015.

Air Education and Training Command Occupational Analysis Division, *Occupational Analysis Report Mental Health Services AFSC 4C0X1 OSSN 3056*, Joint Base San Antonio Randolph, Tex.: Air Force Occupational Analysis Program, 2017.

American Association for Public Opinion Research, "Response Rates— An Overview," webpage, undated. As of November 17, 2021: https://www.aapor.org/Education-Resources/For-Researchers/Poll-Survey-FAQ/Response-Rates-An-Overview.aspx

Amin, Rohul, and Brooke E. Wirtz, "Cognitive Behavioral Therapy for Insomnia Treatment in a Military Deployed Operational Setting Utilizing Enlisted Combat Medics: A Quality and Process Improvement Project," *The Medical Journal (U.S. Army Medical Center of Excellence)*, October– December 2017, pp. 52–59.

Anthony, Jenelle, "Suicide Prevention Spotlight: Military Behavioral Health Technicians," blog post, Military Health System, September 27, 2019. As of November 17, 2021: https://health.mil/Military-Health-Topics/Centers-of-Excellence/ Psychological-Health-Center-of-Excellence/Clinicians-Corner-Blog/ Suicide-Prevention-Spotlight-Military-Behavioral-Health-Technicians

Beidas, Rinad S., and Philip C. Kendall, "Training Therapists in Evidence-Based Practice: A Critical Review of Studies from a Systems-Contextual Perspective," *Clinical Psychology: Science and Practice*, Vol. 17, No. 1, March 2010, pp. 1–30.

Carmer, S. G., and M. R. Swanson, "An Evaluation of Ten Pairwise Multiple Comparison Procedures by Monte Carlo Methods," *Journal of the American Statistical Association*, Vol. 68, No. 341, 1973, pp. 66–74.

Clay, Derrick R., *Medical Education and Training Campus (METC) Behavioral Health Technician Program Curriculum Plan*, Joint Base San Antonio, Tex.: Medical Education and Training Campus, 2016.

Defense Health Agency, *Healthcare Provider's Practice Guide for the Utilization of Behavioral Health Technicians (BHTs)*, Washington, D.C., 2019.

Defense Health Board Task Force on Mental Health, *An Achievable Vision: Report of the Department of Defense Task Force on Mental Health*, Falls Church, Va., June 2007.

Dorvil, Malikah, "2017 Survey of Active Duty Spouses (2017 ADSS)," briefing slides, Alexandria, Va.: U.S. Department of Defense, Office of People Analytics, 2017. As of November 17, 2021:
https://download.militaryonesource.mil/12038/MOS/Surveys/2017-Survey-of-Active-Duty-Spouses-Overview-Briefing.pdf

Frampton, Amanda, "Redefining 'Normal' Mental Health Care Still Means Delivering Quality Patient Care," Air Education and Training Command, May 5, 2020. As of November 17, 2021:
https://www.aetc.af.mil/News/Article/2174882/redefining-normal-mental-health-care-still-means-delivering-quality-patient-care

Griffin, Beth Ann, Greg Ridgeway, Andrew R. Morral, Lane F. Burgette, Craig Martin, Daniel Almirall, Rajeev Ramchand, Lisa H. Jaycox, and Daniel F. McCaffrey, "Toolkit for Weighting and Analysis of Nonequivalent Groups (TWANG)," webpage, RAND Corporation, 2014. As of November 17, 2021:
https://www.rand.org/statistics/twang.html

Harris, Jesse J., and Stacey Berry, "A Brief History of the Military Training of the Enlisted Mental Health Worker," *Journal of Human Behavior in the Social Environment*, Vol. 23, No. 6, 2013, pp. 800–811.

Headquarters U.S. Air Force, Air Force Instruction 44-121, *Alcohol and Drug Abuse Prevention and Treatment (ADAPT) Program*, Washington, D.C., incorporating change 1 and corrective actions, December 19, 2019. As of February 4, 2021:
https://www.hprc-online.org/total-force-fitness/service-specific-resources/air-force/air-force-alcohol-and-drug-abuse

Headquarters, U.S. Department of the Army, Office of the Surgeon General/U.S. Army Medical Command Policy Memo 17-080, *Military Occupational Specialty 68X, Behavioral Health Specialist Utilization*, Joint Base San Antonio, Tex., December 28, 2017; expired December 28, 2019.

Health Care Interservice Training Office, *Behavioral Health Specialist, Behavioral Health Technician, Mental Health Service Apprentice Resource Requirements Analysis Report*, Fort Sam Houston, Tex.: Medical Education and Training Campus, 2015.

Hepner, Kimberly A., Coreen Farris, Carrie M. Farmer, Praise O. Iyiewuare, Terri Tanielian, Asa Wilks, Michael Robbins, Susan M. Paddock, and Harold Alan Pincus, *Delivering Clinical Practice Guideline-Concordant Care for PTSD and Major Depression in Military Treatment Facilities*, Santa Monica, Calif.: RAND Corporation, RR-1692-OSD, 2017. As of November 17, 2021:
https://www.rand.org/pubs/research_reports/RR1692.html

Holliday, Stephanie Brooks, Kimberly A. Hepner, Terri Tanielian, Amanda Meyer, and Harold Alan Pincus, *Understanding Behavioral Health Technicians Within the Military: A Review of Training, Practice, and Professional Development*, Santa Monica, Calif.: RAND Corporation, RR-2649-OSD, 2019. As of November 17, 2021:
https://www.rand.org/pubs/research_reports/RR2649.html

Hoyt, Tim, "Clinical Supervision and Management of US Army Behavioral Health Technicians," *Military Behavioral Health*, Vol. 6, No. 3, 2018, pp. 198–204.

Kellerman, Scott E., and Joan Herold, "Physician Response to Surveys: A Review of the Literature," *American Journal of Preventive Medicine*, Vol. 20, No. 1, January 2001, pp. 61–67.

Krauss, Stacey, and Jillian Ballantyne, "Behavioral Health Technicians: The Unsung Heroes of Training Programs," blog post, Military Health System, 2019. As of November 17, 2021:
https://www.health.mil/Military-Health-Topics/Centers-of-Excellence/
Psychological-Health-Center-of-Excellence/Clinicians-Corner-Blog/
Behavioral-Health-Technicians-The-Unsung-Heroes-of-Training-Programs

Landoll, Ryan R., Matthew K. Nielsen, Kathryn K. Waggoner, and Elizabeth Najera, "Innovations in Primary Care Behavioral Health: A Pilot Study Across the U.S. Air Force," *Translational Behavioral Medicine*, Vol. 9, No. 2, March 2019, pp. 266–273.

Lauver, Kristy J., and Amy Kristof-Brown, "Distinguishing Between Employees' Perceptions of Person-Job and Person-Organization Fit," *Journal of Vocational Behavior*, Vol. 59, No. 3, December 2001, pp. 454–470.

Lytell, Maria C., Susan G. Straus, Chad C. Serena, Geoffrey E. Grimm, James L. Doty III, Jennie W. Wenger, Andrea M. Abler, Andrew M. Naber, Clifford A. Grammich, and Eric S. Fowler, *Assessing Competencies and Proficiency of Army Intelligence Analysts Across the Career Life Cycle*, Santa Monica, Calif.: RAND Corporation, RR-1851-A, 2017. As of November 17, 2021:
https://www.rand.org/pubs/research_reports/RR1851.html

Meadows, Sarah O., Charles C. Engel, Rebecca L. Collins, Robin L. Beckman, Joshua Breslau, Erika Litvin Bloom, Michael Stephen Dunbar, Marylou Gilbert, David Grant, Jennifer Hawes-Dawson, et al., *2018 Department of Defense Health Related Behaviors Survey (HRBS): Results for the Active Component*, Santa Monica, Calif.: RAND Corporation, RR-4222-OSD, 2021. As of November 17, 2021:
https://www.rand.org/pubs/research_reports/RR4222.html

Nielson, Matthew K., *Revolutionizing Mental Health Care Delivery in the United States Air Force by Shifting the Access Point to Primary Care*, unpublished thesis, Maxwell Air Force Base, Ala.: Air Command and Staff College, Air University, 2016.

Ogle, Alan D., J. Brian Rutland, Anna Fedotova, Chad Morrow, Richard Barker, and LaQuanya Mason-Coyner, "Initial Job Analysis of Military Embedded Behavioral Health Services: Tasks and Essential Competencies," *Military Psychology*, Vol. 31, No. 4, 2019, pp. 267–278.

Parsons, Jennifer A., Richard B. Warnecke, Ronald F. Czaja, Janet Barnsley, and Arnold Kaluzny, "Factors Associated with Response Rates in a National Survey of Primary Care Physicians," *Evaluation Review*, Vol. 18, No. 6, December 1994, pp. 756–766.

Potter, Aron, Monty Baker, Carmen Sanders, and Alan Peterson, "Combat Stress Reactions During Military Deployments: Evaluation of the Effectiveness of Combat Stress Control Treatment," *Journal of Mental Health Counseling*, Vol. 31, No. 2, April 1, 2009, pp. 137–148.

Pynes, Joan E., *Human Resources Management for Public and Nonprofit Organizations: A Strategic Approach*, San Francisco, Calif.: John Wiley and Sons, 2009.

Rehmert, Krista, "Behavioral Health Technicians: A Vital Role Supporting the Embedded Behavioral Health Mission," blog post, Military Health System, July 20, 2020. As of November 17, 2021:
https://health.mil/Military-Health-Topics/Centers-of-Excellence/
Psychological-Health-Center-of-Excellence/Clinicians-Corner-Blog/
Behavioral-Health-Technicians-A-Vital-Role-Supporting-the-Embedded-
Behavioral-Health-Mission

Ridgeway, Greg, Daniel F. McCaffrey, Andrew R. Morral, Lane F. Burgette, and Beth Ann Griffin, *Toolkit for Weighting and Analysis of Nonequivalent Groups: A Tutorial for the R TWANG Package*, Santa Monica, Calif.: RAND Corporation, TL-136/1-NIDA, 2014. As of November 17, 2021:
https://www.rand.org/pubs/tools/TL136z1.html

Rock, Lindsay, *Retention Items: Status of Forces Surveys of Active Duty and Reserve Component Members*, Alexandria, Va.: U.S. Department of Defense, Office of People Analytics, February 19, 2020. As of November 17, 2021:
https://dacowits.defense.gov/Portals/48/Documents/General%20Documents/
RFI%20Docs/March2020/OPA%20RFI%206.pdf?ver=2020-03-01-113035-280

Shahmalak, Ujala, Amy Blakemore, Mohammad W. Waheed, and Waquas Waheed, "The Experiences of Lay Health Workers Trained in Task-Shifting Psychological Interventions: A Qualitative Systematic Review," *International Journal of Mental Health Systems*, Vol. 13, 2019, article 64.

Simpson, Scott A., Matthew Goodwin, and Christian Thurstone, "Implementation and Evaluation of a Military-Civilian Partnership to Train Mental Health Specialists," *Military Medicine*, Vol. 184, Nos. 7–8, July–August 2019, pp. e184–e190.

Smith-Forbes, Enrique, Cecilia Najera, and Donald Hawkins, "Combat Operational Stress Control in Iraq and Afghanistan: Army Occupational Therapy," *Military Medicine*, Vol. 179, No. 3, March 2014, pp. 279–284.

Srinivasan, Jayakanth, and Julia DiBenigno, *Site Alpha Behavioral Health System of Care*, Boston, Mass.: Massachusetts Institute of Technology, 2016.

Stratton, Paige C., *Paraprofessional Perceptions of Training and Professional Development*, thesis, Huntington, W.Va.: Marshall University, 2014. As of February 2, 2021:
https://mds.marshall.edu/etd/891

Thomas, Tyrone, "Yokota Medical Group Counters COVID Cases with Augmentee Program," U.S. Air Force, Yokota Air Base, December 2, 2020. As of November 17, 2021:
https://www.yokota.af.mil/News/Article-Display/Article/2433110/yokota-mdg-counters-covid-cases-with-augmentee-program

U.S. Air Force, "Enlisted Mental Health Service," webpage, undated. As of November 17, 2021:
https://www.airforce.com/careers/detail/mental-health-service

———, *AFSC 4C0X1 Mental Health Service Specialty Career Field Education and Training Plan*, Washington, D.C., 2015.

———, *Mental Health Service*, Washington, D.C., 2017.

U.S. Army, "U.S. Army Reserve: Mental Health Specialist (68x)," webpage, undated. As of November 17, 2021:
https://www.goarmy.com/reserve/jobs/browse/medical-and-emergency/mental-health-specialist.html

———, *CMF 68 Smartbook*, Washington, D.C., October 1, 2017.

U.S. Army Training and Doctrine Command, *Soldier's Manual and Trainer's Guide MOS 68X, Behavioral Health Specialist*, Washington, D.C., April 2017.

U.S. Department of Defense, *DoD Survey Burden Action Plan*, Washington, D.C.: Office of the Under Secretary of Defense, Inter-Service Survey Coordinating Committee–Tiger Team, 2015.

U.S. Department of Defense, Office of People Analytics, "2017 Status of Forces Survey of Active Duty Members (SOFS-A)," briefing slides, Alexandria, Va., 2017. As of November 17, 2021:
https://download.militaryonesource.mil/12038/MOS/Surveys/2017-Status-of-Forces-Active-Duty-Briefing.pdf

U.S. Department of Defense and U.S. Department of Veterans Affairs, "Psychological Health Clinical Support Tools," factsheet, Washington, D.C., 2020.

U.S. Department of the Navy, Bureau of Medicine and Surgery Instruction 1510.23D, *Hospital Corpsman Skills Basic*, Falls Church, Va., May 7, 2015.

U.S. Navy, "Job Duty Task Analysis NEC 8485 Mental Health Technician," fact sheet, Washington, D.C., 2013.

————, "Education and Training," *Manual of the Medical Department*, Falls Church, Va., NAVMED P-117, November 1, 2016. As of November 17, 2021: https://www.med.navy.mil/Directives/MANMED

U.S. Navy Personnel Command, "HM NEC Manning Snapshot April 2018," Millington, Tenn., 2018.

U.S. Navy Recruiting Command, "Hospital Corpsman," webpage, undated. As of November 17, 2021: https://www.navy.com/careers/hospital-corpsman

VanGeest, Jonathan B., Timothy P. Johnson, and Verna L. Welch, "Methodologies for Improving Response Rates in Surveys of Physicians: A Systematic Review," *Evaluation and the Health Professions*, Vol. 30, No. 4, January 2008, pp. 303–321.